The Obs
AIF

About the Book

Observers Aircraft is the
guide to the world's late
and most recent version
This, the thirty-sixth an
test fixed-wing and variable-geometry aeroplanes and
rotorcraft of twenty-two countries. Its scope ranges
from such airliner newcomers as the Airbus A320,
through general aviation débutantes as the LET 610,
Seastar and Fokker 100, to such new warplanes as
the Saab Gripen and IAI Lavi. The latest available
information is provided on recently-introduced Soviet
military aircraft, including the MiG-29, and the new-
est variants of such established types as the MiG-23
and Su-24, as well as the latest civil and military aeroplanes now being produced in China. All data has
been checked and revised as necessary, and some
two-thirds of the three-view silhouettes are new or
have been revised.

About the Author

William Green, compiler of *Observers Aircraft* for 36
years, is internationally known for many works of
aviation reference. He entered aviation journalism
during the early years of World War II, subsequently
serving with the RAF and resuming aviation writing
forty years ago, in 1947. Currently managing editor of
one of the largest-circulation European-based aviation journals, *AIR International*, William Green is also
co-editor of *AIR Enthusiast* and the *RAF Yearbook*.

£1.99

KU-283-173

The *Observer's* series was launched in 1937 with the publication of *The Observer's Book of Birds*. Today, fifty years later, paperback *Observers* continue to offer practical, useful information on a wide range of subjects, and with every book regularly revised by experts, the facts are right up-to-date. Students, amateur enthusiasts and professional organisations alike will find the latest *Observers* invaluable.

'Thick and glossy, briskly informative' – *The Guardian*

'If you are a serious spotter of any of the things the series deals with, the books must be indispensable' – *The Times Educational Supplement*

O B S E R V E R S

AIRCRAFT

William Green

With silhouettes by Dennis Punnett

1987 edition

FREDERICK WARNE

FREDERICK WARNE

Penguin Books Ltd, Harmondsworth, Middlesex, England
Viking Penguin Inc., 40 West 23rd Street, New York, New York 10010, U.S.A.
Penguin Books Australia Ltd, Ringwood, Victoria, Australia
Penguin Books Canada Limited, 2801 John Street, Markham, Ontario, Canada
L3R 1B4
Penguin Books (N.Z.) Ltd, 182–190 Wairau Road, Auckland 10, New Zealand

Thirty-sixth edition 1987

Copyright © Frederick Warne & Co., 1987

ISBN 0 7232 3458 2

Printed and bound in Great Britain by Butler & Tanner Ltd, Frome and London

INTRODUCTION TO THE 1987 EDITION

THIRTY-ONE YEARS AGO, two fighters flew for the first time; from certain aspects, both aircraft, the MiG-21 and Mirage III, were epoch marking. Since those mid 'fifties, successive generations of fighters have appeared to be recorded in *Observers Aircraft*, but neither 1956 débutante has been allocated space in this annual publication for a long time. Yet both reappear, albeit in new guises, in the pages of this, the 36th edition: the MiG-21 as an example of Chinese reverse-engineering mated with modern western avionics under the appellation of F-7M Airguard, and the Mirage III now labelled Atlas Cheetah and subject of a major South African mid-life re-engineering and upgrading programme.

Fundamentally products of early 'fifties technology, these aircraft take their place in this volume alongside such newest-generation fighters as the MiG-29, revealed publicly last year, the Israeli Lavi, the Swedish Gripen and the latest variant of the first indigenous Chinese jet fighter, the F-8 II, and such well-established types as the F-14 Tomcat and F-15 Eagle. But Airguard and Cheetah are not the only examples of — by aviation standards — elderly aircraft reappearing in resuscitated form in this edition. The new-production Tu-142M Bear-H has its origins in the early 'fifties Tu-95; the Chinese Y-7-100, appearing in production form late last year, is based on the Antonov An-24 flown in 1960, and the MD-87, latest in the outstandingly successful MD-80 airliner family and included in these pages for the first time, really dates back to the early 'sixties and an original incarnation as the DC-9.

Indeed, two of the past year's most noteworthy commercial *newcomers*, the BAe ATP and Fokker 100, are essentially derivatives of the BAe 748 and the Fellowship, dating back more than two decades with inclusion in many past editions of *Observers Aircraft*. Then there are the -300 "stretches" of such models as the Boeing 767, the BAe 146 and Dash 8, and new turboprop derivatives of piston-engined instructional aircraft, the Aucan and Orlik-Turbo, included in the pages of this volume for the first time. But the foregoing should not lead the reader to suppose that the 1987 edition is devoid of *entirely new* types. On the contrary, such aircraft as the Airbus A320, the CMC Leopard, the Partenavia Mosquito, the PZL Iskierka and the previously-mentioned Saab Gripen make their début to leaven the pages with unfamiliar shapes.

WILLIAM GREEN

AERITALIA-AERMACCHI-EMBRAER AMX

Countries of Origin: Italy and Brazil.
Type: Single-seat battlefield support and light attack aircraft.
Power Plant: One 11,030 lb st (5 000 kgp) Rolls-Royce Spey Mk 807 turbofan.
Performance: Max speed (at 21,164 lb/9 600 kg), 568 mph (913 km/h) at 36,000 ft (10 975 m), or Mach = 0.86, 625 mph (1 005 km/h) at sea level; tactical radius (at 26,896 lb/ 12 200 kg with 5,996-lb/2 720-kg external load and 10 per cent reserve), 322 mls (520 km) HI-LO-HI, 230 mls (370 km) LO-LO-LO; ferry range (with two 220 Imp gal/1 000 l drop tanks), 1,840 mls (2 965 km).
Weights: Operational empty, 14,770 lb (6 700 kg); max take-off, 26,896 lb (12 200 kg).
Armament: (Italian) One 20-mm M61A1 rotary cannon or (Brazilian) two 30-mm DEFA 553 cannon, two AIM-9L Sidewinder or similar AAMs at wingtips and max external ordnance load (including AAMs) of 8,377 lb (3 800 kg).
Status: First prototype flown 15 May 1984. Further three (plus one replacement) prototypes flown in Italy and two additional prototypes flown in Brazil, first of the latter on 16 October 1985. Production of first batch of 30 initiated in July 1986, and current planning calling for 187 and 79 for the Italian and Brazilian air forces respectively. Final assembly lines in both Italy and Brazil, with single-source component manufacture.
Notes: The AMX has been developed jointly by Aeritalia (47.1%) and Aermacchi (23.2%) in Italy, and Embraer (29.7%) in Brazil, and the first deliveries are scheduled for spring 1988. Development of a two-seat operational training version was proceeding at the beginning of 1987.

AERITALIA-AERMACCHI-EMBRAER AMX

Dimensions: Span, 29 ft 1½ in (8,87 m); length, 44 ft 6½ in (13,57 m); height, 15 ft 0¼ in (4,58 m); wing area, 226.05 sq ft (21,00 m²).

AERMACCHI MB-339C

Country of Origin: Italy.
Type: Tandem two-seat advanced trainer and light attack aircraft.
Power Plant: One 4,400 lb st (1 996 kgp) Fiat-built Rolls-Royce Viper 680-43 turbojet.
Performance: Max speed, 561 mph (902 km/h) at sea level, 518 mph (834 km/h) at 36,000 ft (10 975 m); max initial climb (50% fuel), 8,000 ft/min (40,64 m/sec); typical tactical radius (close air support with two 30-mm cannon and two LAU-51 rocket pods, and allowance for 5 min over target), 245 mls (395 km) HI-LO-HI.
Weights: Empty equipped, 7,297 lb (3 310 kg); loaded (pilot training configuration), 10,218 lb (4 635 kg); max take-off, 13,999 lb (6 350 kg).
Armament: (Training and light strike) Two 30-mm cannon in underwing pods included in max of 4,000 lb (1 815 kg) of ordnance distributed between six wing stores stations.
Status: MB-339C flown for first time on 17 December 1985 as latest development of MB-339A, the first of two prototypes of which was flown on 12 August 1976. Initial model supplied to Italian Air Force (100), Dubai (two), Nigeria (12), Malaysia (12) and Peru (16).
Notes: The MB-339C is a progressive development of the MB-339B from which it differs primarily in having a digital navigation/attack system. Whereas the MB-339A has a 4,000 lb st (1 814 kgp) Viper 632-43, the MB-339B introduced the uprated Viper 680-43. The MB-339K is a dedicated single-seat close air support version of the MB-339C with a similar Head-up Display and Nav/Attack system.

AERMACCHI MB-339C

Dimensions: Span (over tip tanks), 36 ft 9¾ in (11,22 m); length, 36 ft 10½ in (11,24 m); height, 12 ft 9½ in (3,90 m); wing area, 207·75 sq ft (19,30 m²).

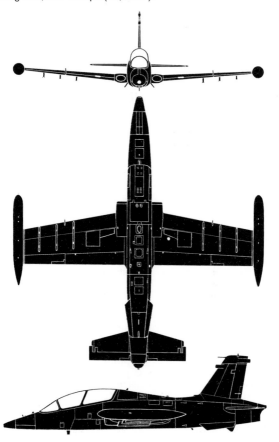

AEROSPATIALE TB 30 EPSILON

Country of Origin: France.

Type: Tandem two-seat primary/basic trainer.

Power Plant: One 300 hp Avco Lycoming AEIO-540-L1B5-D six-cylinder horizontally-opposed engine.

Performance: (At 3,086 lb/1 400 kg) Max speed, 236 mph (380 km/h) at sea level; max cruise (75% power), 222 mph (358 km/h) at 6,000 ft (1 830 m); max initial climb, 1,850 ft/min (9,4 m/sec); service ceiling, 23,000 ft (7 010 m); endurance (60% power), 3·75 hrs.

Weights: Empty equipped, 2,922 lb (917 kg); loaded (aerobatic), 2,756 lb (1 250 kg); max take-off, 3,086 lb (1 400 kg).

Armament: (Export) Four underwing hardpoints stressed to carry 352 lb (160 kg) inboard and 176 lb (80 kg) outboard. Alternative loads include two twin 7,62-mm machine gun pods, four six-rocket (68-mm) pods, or two 264·5-lb (120-kg) bombs.

Status: Two prototypes flown on 22 December 1979 and 12 July 1980 respectively, and first production Epsilon flown on 29 June 1983. The Epsilon joined the *Armée de l'Air* late 1984, and the service has a total requirement for 150 aircraft. Three of the armed export version have been delivered to Togo. Production rate was running at three monthly at the beginning of 1987.

Notes: The first prototype Epsilon has been fitted with a 300 shp Turboméca TP 319 turboprop with which it was first flown on 9 November 1985. This is to serve primarily as a test-bed for the TP 319, but Aérospatiale was considering development of a production version for the export market at the beginning of 1987. The Turbo Epsilon is not expected to differ in any major respect aft of the firewall.

AEROSPATIALE TB 30 EPSILON

Dimensions: Span, 25 ft 11½ in (7,92 m); length, 24 ft 10½ in (7,59 m); height, 8 ft 8¾ in (2,66 m); wing area, 103·34 sq ft (9,60 m²).

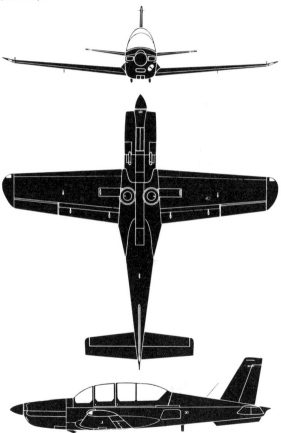

AEROSPATIALE-AERITALIA ATR 42

Countries of Origin: France and Italy.

Type: Regional commercial transport.

Power Plant: Two 1,800 shp Pratt & Whitney Canada PW120 turboprops.

Performance: (ATR 42–300) Max cruise speed, 307 mph (495 km/h) at 20,000 ft (6 095 m); econ cruise, 292 mph (470 km/h) at 25,000 ft (7 620 m); max initial climb, 1,860 ft/min (9,40 m/sec) range (with 46 passengers and reserves), 978 mls (1 575 km) at max cruise at 25,000 ft (6 095 m), (max fuel), 2,647 mls (4 260 km).

Weights: (ATR 42–300) Operational empty, 21,986 lb (9 973 kg); max take-off, 35,605 lb (16 150 kg).

Accommodation: Flight crew of two with optional arrangements for 46, 48 or 50 passengers four abreast.

Status: First of three prototypes flown on 16 August 1984, with certification on 24 September 1985, and first customer deliveries commencing in following November. Total orders for 64 aircraft (plus options on 56) placed by end of December 1986, when production rate was three monthly increasing to four monthly during 1987.

Notes: The ATR (*Avion de Transport Régional*) is manufactured on a 50-50 basis by Aérospatiale of France and Aeritalia of Italy, and is currently being produced in -200 and -300 versions, the former having a gross weight of 34,725 lb (15 750 kg) and lower max landing and zero fuel weights, but both having the same passenger and fuel capacities. A stretched version, the ATR 72 scheduled to enter flight test in the summer of 1988, will have 2,400 shp PW124 engines and accommodate 66–74 passengers. Proposed variants include the ATR 42-F freighter, the ATR 42-S maritime patrol aircraft and the rear-loading ATM-42-R military freighter.

AEROSPATIALE-AERITALIA ATR 42

Dimensions: Span, 80 ft 7½ in (24,57 m); length, 74 ft 5½ in (22,67 m); height, 24 ft 10¾ in (7,59 m); wing area, 586·65 sq ft (54,50 m²).

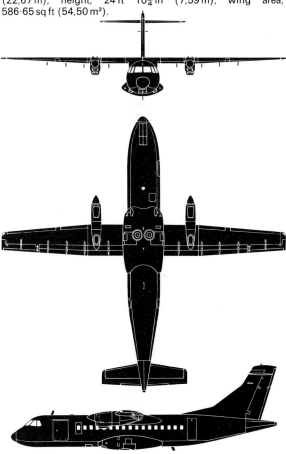

AIRBUS A300-600

Country of Origin: International consortium.

Type: Medium-haul commercial airliner.

Power Plant: Two 56,000 lb st (25 400 kgp) Pratt & Whitney JT9D-7R4H1 or General Electric CF6-80C2 turbofans.

Performance: Max cruise speed, 554 mph (891 km/h) at 31,000 ft (9 450 m); econ cruise, 536 mph (862 km/h) at 33,000 ft (10 060 m); range cruise, 518 mph (833 km/h) at 35,000 ft (10 670 m); range (max payload), 3,430 mls (5 200 km) at econ cruise, (max fuel with 52,900-lb/23 995-kg payload), 5,320 mls (8 560 km).

Weights: Operational empty, 193,410 lb (87 728 kg); max take-off, 363,760 lb (165,000 kg).

Accommodation: Flight crew of three and maximum seating for 344 passengers, a typical arrangement being for 267 passengers in a mixed-class layout.

Status: First JT9D-powered A300-600 flown on 8 July 1983, with first customer delivery (to Saudia) following in May, and first CF6-powered –600 flown on 20 March 1985. Total of 285 A300s (all versions) ordered by December 1986 when 270 delivered. Production rate (including A310) three per month at beginning of 1987.

Notes: The A300 is manufactured by a consortium of Aérospatiale (France), British Aerospace (UK), Deutsche Airbus (Federal Germany) and CASA (Spain). The latest version, the A300-600, replaces the A300B4-200 (see 1983 edition) from which if differs primarily in having the new, re-profiled rear fuselage of the A310 with an extension of the parallel portion of the fuselage offering an 18-seat increase in passenger capacity, and later-generation engines as offered with the A310. The first CF6-80C2-powered -600 was delivered to the launch customer, Thai International, September 1985, and the extended-range A300-600R will fly autumn 1987.

14

AIRBUS A300-600

Dimensions: Span, 147 ft $1\frac{1}{4}$ in (44,84 m); length, 177 ft 5 in (54,08 m); height, 54 ft 3 in (16,53 m); wing area, 2,799 sq ft (260,00 m²).

AIRBUS A310-300

Country of Origin: International consortium.

Type: Medium-range commercial transport.

Power Plant: Two 50,000 lb st (22 680 kg) Pratt & Whitney JT9D-7R4E or General Electric CF6-80C2-A2 turbofans.

Performance: Max cruising speed, 561 mph (903 km/h) at 35,000 ft (10 670 m); long-range cruise, 534 mph (860 km/h) at 37,000 ft (11 280 m); range (with max payload), 4,318 mls (6 950 km) at econ cruise, (max fuel), 6,034 mls (9 710 km) at long-range cruise.

Weights: Operational empty, 169,840 lb (77 040 kg); max take-off, 330,688 lb (150,000 kg).

Accommodation: Flight crew of two or three with 280 passengers with single-class seating eight abreast, or 218 passengers in a typical mixed-class (first and economy) layout.

Status: The first A310-300 was flown on 8 July 1985, and was certified and delivered to launch customer (Swissair) in December 1985, with CF6-powered version being certified in March 1986, with service entry (by Air India) in the following June. First A310 flown on 3 April 1982, and 129 ordered by beginning of December 1986 with 94 delivered. Production rate (including A300—see pages 14–15) three monthly.

Notes: The A310-300 differs from earlier A310 models in having an additional fuel tank in the tailplane, a carbonfibre-reinforced plastic fin, wingtip fences and a revised cockpit. By comparison with the earlier A300B, the A310 has a new, higher aspect ratio wing, a shorter fuselage, a new tailplane and a new undercarriage, but it retains a high degree of commonality with the preceding and larger aircraft. Empty weight of -300 is very similar to -200 despite higher MTOW. The Pratt & Whitney PW4000 will be available as an engine option from mid-1987.

AIRBUS A310-300

Dimensions: Span, 144 ft 0 in (43,90 m); length, 153 ft 1 in (46,66 m); height, 51 ft 10 in (15,81 m); wing area, 2,357·3 sq ft (219,00 m²).

AIRBUS A320-100

Country of Origin: International consortium.

Type: Short- to medium-haul commercial transport.

Power Plant: Two 23,500 lb st (10 660 kgp) General Electric/SNECMA CFM56-5 or IAE V2500 turbofans.

Performance: (Manufacturer's estimates) Max cruise speed, 560 mph (903 km/h) at 28,000 ft (8 535 m); range cruise, 520 mph (840 km/h) at 37,000 ft (11 280 m); range (with 150 passengers), 2,175 mls (3 500 km) at econ cruise.

Weights: Typical operational empty, 84,170 lb (38 180 kg); max take-off, 145,503 lb (66 000 kg).

Accommodation: Flight crew of two and typical mixed-class arrangement for 12 first-class passengers four abreast and 138 economy-class passengers six abreast, or 164 passengers all economy-class.

Status: First of four aircraft to be devoted to flight test was scheduled to fly 21 February 1987, with initial customer deliveries (CFM56–5 engines) in March 1988. V2500-engined version to fly summer 1988, with initial customer deliveries spring 1989. Orders for 246 aircraft (plus 143 options) by December 1986. Production tempo will attain eight aircraft monthly in 1990.

Notes: The world's first fly-by-wire airliner, the A320 is currently being offered in -100 and -200 versions, the latter having additional wing fuel capacity, a max take-off weight of 158,730 lb (72 000 kg) and a range of 3,635 miles (5 850 km) with 150 passengers. Making extensive use of carbon composites and aluminium-lithium in its structure, the A320 features side-stick controllers and fully-integrated large screen cockpit displays.

AIRBUS A320-100

Dimensions: Span, 111 ft 3 in (33,91 m); length, 123 ft 3 in (37,58 m); height, 38 ft 7 in (11,77 m); wing area, 1,317·5 sq ft (122,40 m²).

ANTONOV AN-32 (CLINE)

Country of origin: USSR.

Type: Military tactical transport.

Power Plant: Two 4,195 ehp Ivchenko AI-20M or 5,180 ehp AI-20DM turboprops.

Performance: (AI-20DM engines) Normal continuous cruise, 329 mph (530 km/h) at 26,250 ft (8 000 m); service ceiling, 29,525 ft (9 000 m); range with 45 min reserves (max fuel), 1,367 mls (2 200 km), (max payload), 487 mls (800 km).

Weights: (AI-20DM engines) Max take-off, 59,525 lb (27 000 kg).

Accommodation: Flight crew of five and 39 troops on tip-up seats along fuselage sides, 30 fully-equipped paratroops or 24 casualty stretchers and one medical attendant. A max of 14,770 lb (6 700 kg) of freight may be carried.

Status: Based on the An-26 (Curl), the An-32 was first flown in prototype form late 1976, production of a more powerful version (AI-20DM engines) developed specifically to meet an Indian requirement being initiated in 1982. Deliveries against an Indian order for 95 aircraft commenced in July 1984, and were continuing at the beginning of 1987.

Notes: The AI-20DM-powered An-32 is intended specifically for operation under high temperature conditions or from high-altitude airfields. It features triple-slotted wing trailing-edge flaps and automatic leading-edge slats, and has low-pressure tyres to permit operation from unpaved strips. Named Sutlej (after the Punjabi river) in Indian Air Force service, the An-32 is reported to have been ordered by Tanzania, but the only major customer announced by the beginning of 1987 was India. The An-32 can accommodate various small wheeled or tracked vehicles which may be airdropped.

ANTONOV AN-32 (CLINE)

Dimensions: Span, 95 ft 9½ in (29,20 m); length, 77 ft 8¼ in (23,68 m); height, 28 ft 8½ in (8,75 m); wing area, 807·1 sq ft (74,98 m²).

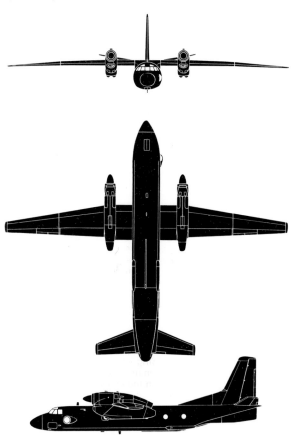

ANTONOV AN-74 (COALER)

Country of Origin: USSR.

Type: STOL arctic survey and (An-72) utility transport aircraft.

Power Plant: Two 14,330 lb st (6 500 kgp) Lotarev D-36 turbofans.

Performance: Max speed, 438 mph (705 km/h); normal cruise, 342 mph (550 km/h); normal operating altitude, 26,245–32,810 ft (8 000–10 000 m); service ceiling, 34,450 ft (10 500 m); range (with 22,045-lb/10 000-kg payload and one hour reserve), 715 mls (1 150 km), (with 11,023-lb/5 000-kg payload and same reserve), 2,050 mls (3 300 km), (with max fuel and 5,070-lb/2 300-kg payload), 2,920 mls (4 700 km).

Weights: Max take-off, 76,058 lb (34 500 kg).

Accommodation: (An-74) Flight crew of four and provisions (between flight deck and freight hold) for eight passengers, or (An-72) flight crew of two and provision for up to 40 passengers on fold-down seats along cabin sides, or up to 26 casualty stretchers plus medical attendants.

Status: The An-72 and An-74 are fundamentally similar, the first of two prototypes of the former flying on 31 August 1977, with pre-production versions of both variants entering test early 1984. Series production reportedly commenced in 1986.

Notes: The An-74 (illustrated) is a dedicated arctic survey version of the An-72 transport from which it differs externally primarily in having observation blisters at the navigator's station on the port side of the fuselage. Both models achieve short take-off and landing (STOL) characteristics by means of upper surface blowing, engine exhaust gases flowing over the upper wing surfaces and inboard slotted flaps.

ANTONOV AN-74 (COALER)

Dimensions: Span, 104 ft 7½ in (31,89 m); length, 92 ft 1 in (26,07 m); height, 28 ft 4½ in (8,65 m).

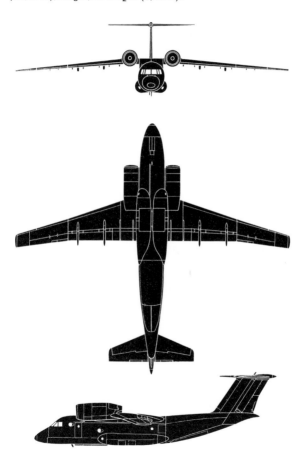

ANTONOV AN-124 RUSLAN (CONDOR)

Country of Origin: USSR.

Type: Heavy strategic freighter.

Power Plant: Four 51,650 lb st (23 430 kgp) Lotarev D.18T turbofans.

Performance: Cruising speed, 497–528 mph (800–850 km/h) at 32,810–39,370 ft (10 000–12 000 m); range (with max payload of 330,688 lb/150 000 kg), 2,796 mls (4 500 km), (max fuel), 10,250 mls (16 500 km).

Weights: Max take-off, 892,857 lb (405 000 kg).

Accommodation: Flight crew of six and upper deck seating for relief crews and up to 88 personnel. Lower deck can accomodate all elements of the SS-20 mobile intermediate-range ballistic missile system, and the largest Soviet tanks and armoured personnel carriers.

Status: First of three prototypes was flown on 26 December 1982, series production being initiated during 1984, with two-three series aircraft delivered by beginning of 1987.

Notes: Named after a character in Russian folklore, the An-124 Ruslan is the world's largest (in terms of wing span) and heaviest aircraft, and, on 26 July 1985, established 21 international records by lifting 377,473 lb (171 219 kg) to 35,269 ft (10 750 m). Advanced features include a fly-by-wire control system, a titanium freight hold floor and extensive use of composites.

ANTONOV AN-124 RUSLAN (CONDOR)

Dimensions: Span, 240 ft 5¾ in (73,30 m); length, 228 ft 0¼ in (69,50 m); height, 73 ft 9¾ in (22,50 m); wing area, 6,760 sq ft (628 m²).

ARV SUPER2

Country of Origin: United Kingdom.
Type: Side-by-side two-seat club and training aircraft.
Power Plant: One 77 hp Hewland Engineering AE75 three-cylinder two-stroke engine.
Performance: Max speed, 126 mph (202 km/h) at 3,500 ft (1 065 m); cruise, 110 mph (177 km/h) at 3,500 ft (1 065 m); max initial climb, 670 ft/min (3,4 m/sec); max range (with 45 min reserve), 267 mls (430 km) at 95 mph (154 km/h).
Weights: Empty, 640 lb (290 kg); max take-off, 1,100 lb (499 kg).
Status: First of two prototypes flown 11 March 1985, with certificate of airworthiness obtained in September 1986, and some 20 completed by the beginning of 1987. The Super2 is being offered both flyaway and in 65 per cent assembled kit form.
Notes: Claimed to be the first wholly original all-British light engine-airframe combination for "several decades", the Super2 utilises original production techniques. Apart from glassfibre wingtips, fairings and cowlings, it is primarily of aluminium construction and is of conventional design, except for the five degrees of forward wing rake. Claimed to reduce primary instructional costs by 25 per cent, the Super2 has detachable wings to facilitate road transportation and reduce storage costs. Volume production is expected to commence during the course of 1987, with a peak production of five-six weekly anticipated.

ARV SUPER2

Dimensions: Span, 28 ft 6 in (8,69 m); length, 18 ft 0 in (5,49 m); height, 7 ft 8 in (2,34 m); wing area, 92·5 sq ft (8,59 m²).

ATLAS CHEETAH

Country of Origin: South Africa (France).
Type: Single-seat multi-role fighter and two-seat conversion trainer.
Power Plant: One 9,346 lb st (4 280 kgp) dry and 13,670 lb st (6 200 kgp) reheat SNECMA Atar 9C turbojet.
Performance: (Estimated) Max speed, 850 mph at sea level, or Mach = 1·115, 1,460 mph (2 350 km/h) at 36,000 ft (10 975 m), or Mach = 2·21; time to 36,000 ft (10 975 m), 3·0 min; service ceiling (at Mach = 1·8), 55,775 ft (17 000 m).
Weights: (Estimated) Empty, 16,000 lb (7 258 kg); max take-off, 30,000 lb (13 608 kg).
Armament: Two 30-mm DEFA cannon and (air-air mission) up to four Armscor Kukri AAMs, or (air-ground mission) mix of CB470 cluster bombs or Mk 82 bombs on four external stations.
Status: A mid-life upgrade of the Dassault-Breguet Mirage III (in which approximately 50 per cent of the aircraft is reconstructed), the Cheetah was first revealed on 16 July 1986. The prototype is converted from a Mirage IIID2Z two-seat trainer, and initially some 30 single-seat Mirage IIIEZs are undergoing similar conversion. Later, additional Mirage IIID2Zs, single-seat IIICZs and IIIR2Zs, and, possibly, two-seat IIIBZs are expected to be rotated through the programme.
Notes: The Cheetah is a reconstructed version of single- and two-seat (illustrated) Mirages with improved radar, an integrated nav/attack system with laser designator, a Doppler navigation system (in place of INS) and canards to enhance agility.

ATLAS CHEETAH

Dimensions: (Two-seat version) Span, 27 ft 0 in (8,22 m); length (including probe), 53 ft 6 in (16,3 m); height, 14 ft 9 in (4,50 m); wing area, 375 sq ft (34,85 m²).

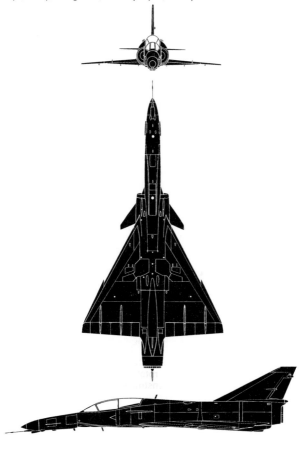

BEECHCRAFT BEECHJET

Country of Origin: USA (Japan).
Type: Light corporate executive transport.
Power Plant: Two 2,900 lb st (1 315 kgp) Pratt & Whitney Canada JT15D-5 turbofans.
Performance: Max Speed, 520 mph (837 km/h), or Mach = 0·785; typical speed at 39,000 ft (11 890 m), 465 mph (748 km/h); initial climb, 3,960 ft/min (20,12 m/sec); ceiling, 41,000 ft (12 495 m); max range (with four passengers and IFR reserves), 1,760 mls (2 832 km), (with VFR reserves), 2,220 mls (3 572 km).
Weights: Basic operational, 9,315 lb (4 225 kg); max take-off, 15,780 lb (7 158 kg).
Accommodation: Pilot and co-pilot on flight deck and standard arrangement in main cabin for seven passengers, with four seats in facing pairs and a three-place sofa.
Status: The Beechjet is a derivative of the Mitsubishi Diamond 2, the manufacturing rights in which have been acquired from the Japanese company by the Beech Aircraft Corporation. Four of five Diamond 2s acquired by Beech were modified as Beechjets during 1986, and the first Beech-assembled aircraft was completed in August of that year. Production was being raised from one to two aircraft monthly at the beginning of 1987.
Notes: The Beechjet is basically a re-engined version of the Mitsubishi Diamond 2 embodying a new interior and various refinements. A progressive development of the Diamond I and IA, the Diamond 2 was first flown on 20 June 1984, the first production aircraft flying on 28 January 1985. Eleven were produced by Mitsubishi of which six were sold, the remainder being acquired by Beech.

BEECHCRAFT BEECHJET

Dimensions: Span, 43 ft 6 in (13,25 m); length, 48 ft 5 in (14,75 m); height, 13 ft 9 in (4,19 m); wing area, 241·4 sq ft (22,43 m²).

BEECHCRAFT 2000 STARSHIP 1

Country of Origin: USA.
Type: Light corporate executive transport.
Power Plant: Two 1,100 shp Pratt & Whitney Canada PT6A-67 turboprops.
Performance: Max cruise speed, 405 mph (652 km/h) at 25,000 ft (7 620 m); econ cruise, 313 mph (504 km/h) at 39,000 ft (11 885 m); max initial climb, 3,248 ft/min (16,50 m/sec); certified ceiling, 41,000 ft (12 495 m); max fuel range (45 min reserves), 3,020 mls (4 860 km), (max payload with 45 min reserves), 1,298 mls (2 089 km).
Weights: (Estimated) Empty equipped, 8,800 lb (3 992 kg); max take-off, 14,000 (6 350 kg).
Accommodation: Provision for two crew on flight deck and max of 10 passengers in main cabin. Six basic interior configurations offered, a typical arrangement providing seven single seats and a two-place divan.
Status: First of three prototypes of the Starship flown on 15 February 1986, this being preceded (on 29 August 1983) by an 85 per cent scale proof-of-concept vehicle. Certification scheduled for the end of 1987, with customer deliveries expected to begin in the second quarter of 1988.
Notes: The Starship is innovative in concept in that it mates an aft-mounted laminar-flow wing with a variable-sweep foreplane, the sweep being changed with flap extension to provide fully-automatic pitch-trim compensation. Extensive use is made in the structure of such materials as boron, carbon, Kevlar and glassfibre, but the incorporation of design changes has resulted in empty weight growth and a year's delay in certification and initial customer deliveries. The 1,000 shp PT6A-27 engines originally planned have now given place to PT6A-67s.

BEECHCRAFT 2000 STARSHIP 1

Dimensions: Span, 54 ft 0 in (16,46 m); length, 46 ft 1 in (14,05 m); height, 12 ft 10 in (3,91 m); wing area, 280·9 sq ft (26,09 m²).

BOEING 737-300

Country of Origin: USA.

Type: Short-haul commercial airliner.

Power Plant: Two 20,000 lb st (9 072 kgp) General Electric CFM56-3-B1 turbofans.

Performance: Max cruising speed, 558 mph (899 km/h) at 25,000 ft (7 620 m); econ cruise, 489 mph (787 km/h) at 35,000 ft (10 670 m); range cruise, 495 mph (797 km/h) at 35,000 ft (10 670 m); max range at econ cruise (max payload), 2,625 mls (4 225 km), (max fuel), 3,408 mls (5 485 km).

Weights: Operational empty, 69,580 lb (31 561 kg); max take-off, 135,000 lb (61 236 kg).

Accommodation: Flight crew of two and alternative arrangements for 110 to 149 passengers, typical arrangements including mixed class with four-abreast seating for eight first class and six-abreast seating for 114 or 120 tourist class passengers, or one class arrangement for 132, 140 or 149.

Status: First Model 737-300 flown on 24 February 1984, with second on 2 March 1984. First customer delivery (to US Air) 28 November 1984, and total of 546 ordered by December 1986, when 1,736 of all versions of the Model 737 had been ordered and production was 14·5 monthly.

Notes: The Model 737-300 differs from the -200 (see 1983 edition) in having new engines, a 104-in (2,64-m) overall "stretch", strengthened wings and modified wingtips. The -300 is not simply a stretched and re-engined version of the Model 737 as it embodies many of the developments made available by the Model 757 and 767 programmes, and it is seen as complementary to the Model 737-200. The 737-400, for late 1988 delivery, will have a further 114-in (2,89-m) "stretch", 22,000 lb st (9 979 kgp) CFM56-3-B2 engines and a 138,000 lb (62 597 kg) max take-off weight.

34

BOEING 737-300

Dimensions: Span, 94 ft 9 in (28,90 m); length, 109 ft 7 in (33,40 m); height, 36 ft 6 in (11,12 m); wing area, 980 sq ft (91,04 m²).

BOEING 747-300

Country of Origin: USA.

Type: Long-haul commercial airliner.

Power Plant: Four 54,750 lb st (24 835 kgp) Pratt & Whitney JT9D-7R4G2 turbofans.

Performance: Max cruise speed, 583 mph (939 km/h) at 35,000 ft (10 670 m); econ cruise, 564 mph (907 km/h) at 35,000 ft (10 670 m); long-range cruise, 558 mph (898 km/h); range (max payload at econ cruise), 6,860 mls (11 040 km), (max fuel at long-range cruise), 8,606 mls (13 850 km).

Weights: Operational empty, 389,875 lb (176 847 kg); max take-off, 833,000 lb (377 850 kg).

Accommodation: Normal flight crew of three and up to 69 passengers six-abreast on upper deck, plus basic mixed-class arrangement for 410 passengers, or 415 passengers nine-abreast or 484 10-abreast in economy class seating.

Status: First Model 747-300 flown on 5 October 1982, with first customer delivery (Swissair) March 1983. Total of 764 of all versions of the Model 747 ordered by the beginning of November 1986, with 655 delivered and production running at two per month.

Notes: The Model 747-300 differs from the -200 primarily in having a 23-ft (7,0-m) lengthening of the upper deck affording a (typical) 10 per cent increase in total accommodation. Boeing is offering to convert existing Model 747s to -300 standard. The first Model 747-100 was flown on 9 February 1969, and the first Model 747-200 on 11 October 1970. On 22 October 1985, a launch order was announced for 10 of the Model 747-400. The -400, which will enter test in the first quarter of 1988, will use 56,000 lb st (25 400 kgp) PW4256, RB211-524D4D or CF6-80C2 engines and will have a gross weight of up to 850,000 lb (385 560 kg). It will feature extended wingtips and winglets, a two-crew flight deck and make extensive use of new materials.

BOEING 747-300

Dimensions: Span, 195 ft 8 in (59,64 m); length, 231 ft 4 in (70,51 m); height, 63 ft 5 in (19,33 m); wing area, 5,685 sq ft (528,15 m²).

BOEING 757-200

Country of Origin: USA.

Type: Short/medium-haul commercial airliner.

Power Plant: Two 37,500 lb st (17 010 kgp) Rolls-Royce RB.211-535C, 38,200 lb st (17 327 kgp) Pratt & Whitney 2037 or 40,100 lb st (18 190 kgp) Rolls-Royce RB.211-535E4 turbofans.

Performance: (RB.211-535C engines) Max cruise speed, 570 mph (917 km/h) at 30,000 ft (9 145 m); econ cruise, 528 mph (850 km/h) at 39,000 ft (11 885 m); range (max payload), 2,210 mls (3 556 km) at econ cruise, (max fuel), 5,343 mls (8 598 km) at long-range cruise.

Weights: Operational empty, 128,450 lb (58 265 kg); max take-off (RB.211-535C engines), 220,000 lb (99 790 kg).

Accommodation: Flight crew of two (with provision for optional third crew member) and typical arrangement of 178 mixed class or 196 tourist class passengers, with max single-class seating for 239 passengers.

Status: First Model 757 flown on 19 February 1982, with first customer deliveries (to Eastern) December 1982 and (British Airways) January 1983. Orders totalling 196 aircraft by December 1986, with deliveries with Pratt & Whitney engines having commenced (to Delta Air Lines) October 1984. Production rate of two-and-a-half aircraft monthly at beginning of 1987, with total of 115 delivered.

Notes: Two versions of the Model 757 are currently on offer, one with a max take-off weight of 220,000 lb (99 790 kg) and the other with a max take-off weight of 240,000 lb (108 864 kg). The Model 757 is of narrowbody configuration and its wing has been optimised for short-haul routes. At the beginning of 1987, Boeing was offering the extended-range 757ER (deliveries of which commenced in May 1986), the 757PF freighter and the Model 757-200 Combi.

BOEING 757-200

Dimensions: Span, 124 ft 6 in (37,82 m); length, 155 ft 3 in (47,47 m); height, 44 ft 6 in (13,56 m); wing area, 1,951 sq ft (181,25 m²).

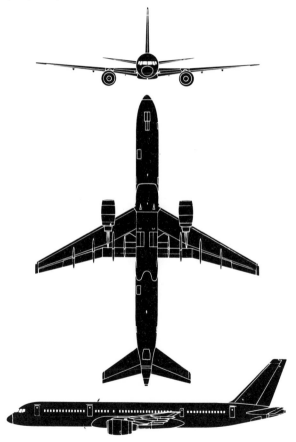

BOEING 767-300

Country of Origin: USA.

Type: Medium-haul commercial airliner.

Power Plant: Two 50,000 lb st (22 680 kgp) Pratt & Whitney JT9D-7R4E or General Electric CF6-80A2 turbofans.

Performance: (CF6-80A2 engines) Max cruise speed, 557 mph (897 km/h) at 39,000 ft (11 890 m); econ cruise, 528 mph (850 km/h) at 39,000 ft (11 890 m); range (with max payload), 3,520 mls (5 665 km) at econ cruise, (max fuel), 5,780 mls (9 305 km) at long-range cruise.

Weights: (CF6-80A-2 engines) Operational empty, 187,900 lb (85 231 kg); max take-off, 351,000 lb (159 213 kg).

Accommodation: Flight crew of two and typical mixed-class seating for 24 first-class passengers six-abreast and 237 tourist-class passengers seven-abreast with two aisles.

Status: First Model 767 flown on 26 September 1981, with first customer delivery (to United) on 18 August 1982. First -300 flown on 1 February 1986, and first customer delivery (to Japan Air Lines) on 25 September 1986. Total of 211 (all models) ordered by end of December 1986, including 27 -300s, with 158 delivered.

Notes: The -300 version of the Model 767 differs from the -200 (see 1986 edition) in embodying a 21·25-ft (6,48-m) fuselage stretch. Under development are the -300ER (Extended Range) and -300LR (Long Range) versions. The former will have a gross weight of 380,000 lb (172 365 kg), later increasing to 400,000 lb (181 440 kg), with 56,000 lb st (25 400 kgp) PW 4000 or CF6-80C2 engines. At the beginning of 1987, a -400 version with an additional fuselage stretch of approx 10 ft (3,00 m) and providing about 28 more seats was under consideration, this having a range of 5,295-5,990 mls (8 520–9 640 km).

40

BOEING 767-300

Dimensions: Span, 156 ft 1 in (47,60 m); length, 180 ft 3 in (54,94 m); height, 52 ft 0 in (15,85 m); wing area, 3,050 sq ft (283,3 m²)

BOEING E-3 SENTRY

Country of Origin: USA.
Type: Airborne warning and control system aircraft.
Power Plant: Four 21,000 lb st (9 525 kgp) Pratt & Whitney TF33-PW-100A turbofans.
Performance: (At max weight) Average cruise speed, 479 mph (771 km/h) at 28,900-40,100 ft (8 810-12 220 m); average loiter speed, 376 mph (605 km/h) at 29,000 ft (8 840 m); time on station (unrefuelled) at 1,150 mls (1 850 km) from base, 6 hrs, (with one refuelling), 14·4 hrs; ferry range, 5,034 mls (8 100 km) at 475 mph (764 km/h).
Weights: Empty, 170,277 lb (77 238 kg); normal loaded, 214,300 lb (97 206 kg); max take-off, 325,000 lb (147 420 kg).
Accommodation: Operational crew of 17 comprising flight crew of four, systems maintenance team of four, a battle commander and an air defence team of eight.
Status: First of two (EC-137D) development aircraft flown 9 February 1972, two pre-production E-3As following in 1975. First 24 delivered to USAF as E-3As have been modified to E-3B standards, and final 10 (including updated third test aircraft) were delivered as E-3Cs. Eighteen were delivered (in similar configuration to E-3C) to NATO as E-3As with completion April 1985. Five CFM56-powered aircraft being sent to Saudi Arabia between August 1985 and March 1987 and six (plus two on option) to be supplied to the RAF in 1991.
Notes: Aircraft initially delivered to USAF as E-3As have now been fitted with JTIDS (Joint Tactical Information Distribution System), ECM-resistant voice communications, additional HF and UHF radios, austere maritime surveillance capability and more situation display consoles as E-3Bs. The E-3C featured most E-3B modifications at the production stage. The CFM56-powered E-3 for Saudi Arabia is illustrated above.

BOEING E-3 SENTRY

Dimensions: Span, 145 ft 9 in (44,42 m); length, 152 ft 11 in (46,61 m); height, 42 ft 5 in (12,93 m); wing area, 2,892 sq ft (268,67 m²).

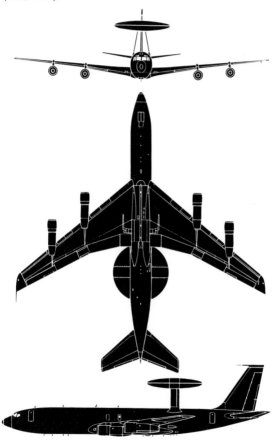

BRITISH AEROSPACE 125-800

Country of Origin: United Kingdom.
Type: Light corporate executive transport.
Power Plant: Two 4,300 lb st (1 950 kgp) Garrett TFE371-5R-1H turbofans.
Performance: Max cruise speed, 525 mph (845 km/h) at 29,000 ft (8 840 m); econ cruise, 461 mph (741 km/h) at 39,000–43,000 ft (11 900–13 100 m); max initial climb, 3,100 ft/min (15,75 m/sec); service ceiling, 43,000 ft (13 100 m); range (max payload), 3,305 mls (5 318 km), (max fuel with VFR reserves), 3,454 mls (5 560 km).
Weights: Typical operational empty, 15,120 lb (6 858 kg); max take-off, 27,400 lb (12 430 kg).
Accommodation: Flight crew of two (with provision for third crew member on flight deck) and standard arrangement for eight passengers in main cabin, with optional arrangements for up to 14 passengers.
Status: Prototype of Series 800 BAe 125 flown on 26 May 1983, with initial customer deliveries commencing in the following year. Production rate of two aircraft monthly during 1986, with 71 Series 800s ordered by January 1987.
Notes: The BAe 125–800 is an extensively revised development of the Series 700 (see 1982 edition) with more powerful engines, new, longer-span outboard wing sections, new ailerons, redesigned flight deck and larger ventral fuel tank. During the course of 1986, a new luggage area increasing luggage capacity from 44 to 52 cu ft (1,25 to 1,47 m³) was introduced, and thrust reversers were offered as an option. Sales of earlier turbojet- and turbofan-powered models of the BAe 125 totalled 573 aircraft, including 215 of the Series 700 aircraft. The BAe 125 serves in crew training, aeromedical and airways calibration roles as well as that of corporate transport.

BRITISH AEROSPACE 125-800

Dimensions: Span, 51 ft 4½ in (15,66 m); length, 51 ft 2 in (15,59 m); height, 17 ft 7 in (5,37 m); wing area, 374 sq ft (32,75 m²).

BRITISH AEROSPACE 146-300

Country of Origin: United Kingdom.
Type: Short-haul regional airliner.
Power Plant: Four 6,970 lb st (3 161 kgp) Avco Lycoming ALF 502R-5 turbofans.
Performance: (Manufacturer's estimates) Econ cruise speed, 439 mph (707 km/h) at 30,000 ft (9 145 m); range (with 100 passengers and reserves for 173-mile/278-km diversion plus 45 min at 5,000 ft/1 525 m), 1,255 mls (2 020 km) at long-range cruise; ferry range (standard fuel), 1,750 mls (2 817 km).
Weights: Operational empty, 54,000 lb (24 494 kg); max take-off, 93,000 lb (42 185 kg).
Accommodation: Flight crew of two and 110 passengers six abreast or 100 passengers five abreast, with optional mixed-class arrangements (eg, 35 business and 65 economy class, or 10 first and 84 economy-class).
Status: Aerodynamic prototype (conversion of Srs 100 prototype) scheduled to fly May 1987, with first customer deliveries (to Air Wisconsin) during last quarter of 1988. Orders for all versions of the BAe 146 totalled 78 aircraft (plus 30 options) by December 1986. Some 60 had been delivered by the beginning of 1987.
Notes: The Series 300 version of the BAe 146 differs from the current production Series 200 primarily in having a 7 ft 10 in (2,39 m) fuselage stretch by means of plugs fore and aft of the wing. Extra internal cabin width has been achieved by modification of the fuselage frame profile. A freighter version of the Series 200, the BAe 146-QT (Quiet Trader) is projected, together with governmental transport versions of both Series 100 and 200 as the Statesman.

BRITISH AEROSPACE 146-300

Dimensions: Span, 86 ft 5 in (26,34 m); length, 101 ft 8 in (30,99 m); height, 28 ft 3 in (8,61 m); wing area, 832 sq ft (77,30 m²).

BRITISH AEROSPACE ATP

Country of Origin: United Kingdom.
Type: Regional commercial transport.
Power Plant: Two 2,150 shp (2,400 shp emergency) Pratt & Whitney Canada PW124 or (2,500 shp emergency) PW125 turbo-props.
Performance: (Manufacturer's estimates) Max cruise speed, 306 mph (492 km/h) at 15,000 ft (4 670 m); econ cruise, 301 mph (485 km/h) at 18,000 ft (5 485 m); typical initial climb, 1,370 ft/min (6,96 m/sec); max operating altitude, 25,000 ft (7 620 m); range (max payload), 980 mls (1 576 km) at econ cruise, (max fuel and 8,330-lb/3 778-kg payload), 2,725 mls (4 386 km) at long-range cruise.
Weights: Typical operational empty, 29,970 lb (13 594 kg); max take-off, 49,500 lb (22 453 kg).
Accommodation: Flight crew of two and standard configuration for 64 passengers four abreast, with optional high-density arrangement for 72 passengers.
Status: Prototype flown on 6 August 1986, with customer deliveries (to British Midland) scheduled to commence in September 1987. Orders for five aircraft (plus four options) placed by end of December 1986.
Notes: The ATP (the initials signifying "Advanced Turboprop") is technically a stretched development of the BAe 748, but apart from lengthened fuselage, it embodies new engines, systems and equipment, swept vertical tail surfaces and a redesigned nose. Other modifications include revised cockpit, window and door arrangements. The ATP is the only new-generation regional turboprop capable of using jetways at major airports.

BRITISH AEROSPACE ATP

Dimensions: Span, 100 ft 6 in (30,63 m); Length, 85 ft 4 in (26,01 m); height, 23 ft 5 in (7,14 m); wing area, 842·84 sq ft (78,30 m²).

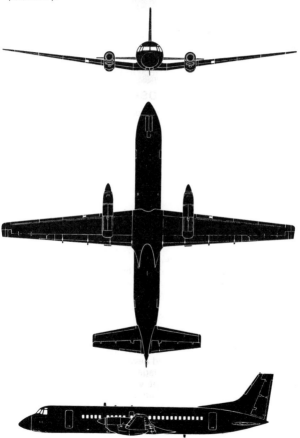

BRITISH AEROSPACE EAP

Country of Origin: United Kingdom.
Type: Single-seat advanced fighter technology demonstrator.
Power Plant: Two (approx) 9,000 lb st (4 082 kgp) dry and 16,500 lb st (7 484 kgp) reheat Turbo-Union RB199-34R Mk 104D turbofans.
Performance: No details have been released for publication but it is assumed that max speed exceeds 1,320 mph (2 124 km/h), or Mach = 2·0, above 36,000 ft (10 975 m).
Weights: Empty (approx), 22,050 lb (10 000 kg); loaded (clean), (approx) 32,000 lb (14 515 kg).
Armament: (Typical) Four BAe Sky Flash (two beneath fuselage and two beneath wing roots) and two AIM-9L Sidewinder (at wingtips) AAMs.
Status: Single example flown for first time on 8 August 1986.
Notes: The EAP (Experimental Aircraft Programme) technology demonstrator is intended to investigate high AOA (Angle of Attack) operation and other flight characteristics demanded of the next generation of fighters, and other basic new technologies. These include advanced structural design with extensive use of carbonfibre composites, active fly-by-wire controls and an advanced electronic cockpit. The EAP is providing data for the EFA (European Fighter Aircraft) being developed by Eurofighter GmbH (formed by the UK, Germany, Italy and Spain). The EFA is of fundamentally similar configuration to that of the EAP, but smaller and lighter, with a basic mass empty weight of 20,945 lb (9 500 kg) and a 53-deg delta wing of 34·45 ft (10,50 m) span and 538·2 sq ft (50,000 m²) area. The EAP is not intended for weapons systems demonstration, but makes provision for the carriage of missiles as described above. Fifty-two flights had been completed by the beginning of 1987, when the aircraft was being fitted with an updated flight control system for increased incidence/aft CG handling.

BRITISH AEROSPACE EAP

Dimensions: Span, 36 ft 7¾ in (11,17 m); length (over probe), 48 ft 2¾ in (14,70 m); height, 18 ft 1⅛ in (5,52 m); wing area, 560 sq ft (52,00 m²).

BRITISH AEROSPACE HARRIER GR MK 5

Countries of Origin: United Kingdom and USA.
Type: Single-seat V/STOL close support and tactical reconnaissance aircraft.
Power Plant: One (short lift wet) 21,180 lb st (9 607 kgp)
and (combat) 18,750 lb st (8 505 kgp) Rolls-Royce Pegasus
Mk 105 vectored-thrust turbofan.
Performance: Max speed (clean), 647 mph (1 041 km/h) at
sea level, or Mach=0·85, 600 mph (966 km/h) at 36,000 ft,
or Mach=0·91; tactical radius (interdiction with seven Mk 82
bombs, 25-mm cannon and two 250 Imp gal/1 136 l drop
tanks), 553 mls (889 km) HI-LO-HI; ferry range (with four 250
Imp gal/1 136 l external tanks), 2,440 mls (3 927 km).
Weights: Operational empty, 13,798 lb (6 258 kg); max
take-off VTO (ISA), 18,950 lb (8 595), STO, 29,750 lb
(13 495 kg).
Armament: Two 25-mm cannon (on under-fuselage
stations) and up to 16 Mk 82 or six Mk 83 bombs, six BL-
755 cluster bombs, four Maverick ASMs, or ten rocket pods
on six wing stations. Max external load, 9,200 lb (4 173 kg).
Status: First of two (weapon system) development aircraft
flown on 30 April 1985, with deliveries to RAF against initial
order for 60 series aircraft commencing in 1987. Long lead
items ordered for further 27 aircraft by late 1986.
Notes: The Harrier GR Mk 5 is the RAF equivalent of the US
Marine Corps' AV-8B Harrier II, airframe production being
divided between British Aerospace and McDonnell Douglas.
The USMC has a requirement for 328 AV-8Bs of which 28
are being supplied as tandem two-seat TAV-8Bs (see pages
138-9) for instructional purposes. Twelve are on order for the
Spanish Navy (as EAV-8Bs). The AV-8B version carries a
single five-barrel 25-mm cannon, and nocturnal under-the-
weather capability is being introduced.

BRITISH AEROSPACE HARRIER GR MK5

Dimensions: Span, 30 ft 4 in (9,24 m); length, 46 ft 4 in (14,12 m); height, 11 ft 7¾ in (3,55 m); wing area, 230 sq ft (21,37 m²).

BRITISH AEROSPACE HAWK 200

Country of Origin: United Kingdom.
Type: Single-seat multi-role fighter.
Power Plant: One 5,845 lb st (2 650 kgp) Rolls-Royce Turboméca Adour 871 turbofan.
Performance: Max speed, 645 mph (1 037 km/h) at 8,000 ft (2 440 m), or Mach = 0·87; service ceiling, 50,000 ft (15 240 m); tactical radius (LO-LO close air support), 200 mls (322 km) with eight 500-lb/227-kg bombs, 120 mls (193 km) with five 1,000-lb/454-kg and four 500-lb/227-kg bombs, (HI-LO-HI interdiction), 667 mls (1 073 km) with 3,000-lb (1 360-kg) warload; ferry range (with two 190 Imp gal/ 860 l and one 130 Imp gal/590 l tanks), 2,240 mls (3 606 km).
Weights: Empty, 9,100 lb (4 127 kg); max take-off, 19,000 lb (8 618 kg).
Armament: Two 25-mm Aden or 27-mm Mauser cannon and max external warload of 7,700 lb (3 493 kg) on centreline and four wing stations.
Status: First prototype flown on 19 May 1986 (this being lost in an accident on 2 July) with pre-production aircraft to fly during May 1987.
Notes: The Hawk 200 is a dedicated single-seat combat derivative of the two-seat Hawk basic/advanced trainer and light tactical aircraft (see 1985 edition and pages 136-7 of this edition), sharing with the two-seat Hawk 100 the Adour 871 which replaces the 5,200 lb st (2 359 kgp) Adour 151 of the RAF's Hawk T Mk 1, and the 5,340 lb st (2 422 kgp) Adour 851 and 5,700 lb st (2 585 kgp) Adour 861 of the export Hawk 50 and 60 respectively. The Hawk 200 retains some 80 per cent commonality with the Hawk 100 with which it shares an inertial navigator, head-up display, laser range-finder and weapon aiming computer.

BRITISH AEROSPACE HAWK 200

Dimensions: Span, 30 ft 9¾ in (9,39 m); length, 37 ft 4 in (11,30 m); height, 13 ft 8 in (4,15 m); wing area, 179·64 sq ft (16,69 m²).

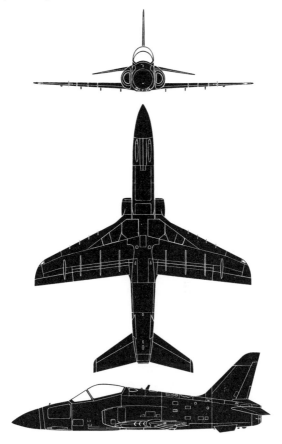

BRITISH AEROSPACE JETSTREAM 31

Country of Origin: United Kingdom.
Type: Light regional airliner and corporate transport.
Power Plant: Two 940 shp Garrett TPE331–10 turboprops.
Performance: Max cruise speed, 299 mph (482 km/h) at 20,000 ft (6 100 m); long-range cruise, 265 mph (426 km/h) at 25,000 ft (7 620 m); initial climb, 2,200 ft/min (11,2 m/sec); max range (with 19 passengers and IFR reserves), 737 mls (1 186 km), (with 12 passengers), 1,094 mls (1 760 km), (with nine passengers), 1,324 mls (2 130 km).
Weights: Operational empty, 9,613 lb (4 360 kg); max take-off, 15,322 lb (6 950 kg).
Accommodation: Flight crew of two and commuter airliner arrangement for 18–19 passengers three abreast, or basic corporate executive seating for eight passengers and optional 12-seat executive shuttle arrangement.
Status: First Jetstream 31 flown on 18 March 1982, following flight development aircraft (converted from Series 1 airframe) flown on 28 March 1980. First customer delivery (Contactair) made 15 December 1982, and 130 aircraft sold (with 26 options) to 20 operators in seven countries by end of December 1986, when production tempo was four aircraft monthly.
Notes: The Jetstream 31 is a derivative of the Handley Page H.P.137 Jetstream, the original prototype of which was flown on 18 August 1967. Apart from four aircraft for Royal Navy observer training with ASR 360 radar (Jetstream T Mk 3s), all aircraft of this type so far sold have been of the basic "Commuter" configuration. A stretched version for 24–27 passengers was under consideration at the beginning of 1987, together with the Jetstream 31EZ for offshore patrol and surveillance.

BRITISH AEROSPACE JETSTREAM 31

Dimensions: Span, 52 ft 0 in (15,85 m); length, 47 ft 2 in (14,37 m); height, 17 ft 6 in (5,37 m); wing area, 270 sq ft (25,08 m²).

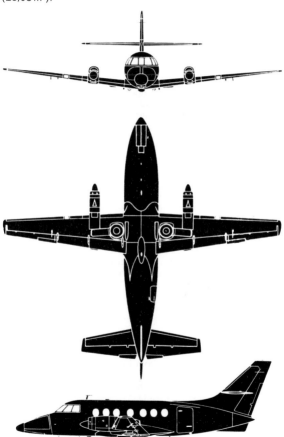

BRITISH AEROSPACE SEA HARRIER

Country of Origin: United Kingdom.
Type: Single-seat V/STOL shipboard multirole fighter.
Power Plant: One 21,500 lb st (9 760 kgp) Rolls-Royce Pegasus 104 vectored-thrust turbofan.
Performance: Max speed (clean aircraft), 720 mph (1 160 km/h) at 1,000 ft (305 m), or Mach=0·95, 607 mph (977 km/h) at 36,000 ft (10 975 m), or Mach=0·92, (with two each Martel ASMs and AIM-9L AAMs), 598 mph (962 km/h) at sea level, or Mach=0·83; tactical radius (recce mission with two 100 Imp gal/455 l drop tanks), 323 mls (520 km); endurance (combat air patrol with two drop tanks and allowance for 3 min combat), 1·5 hrs at 115 mls (185 km) from carrier.
Weights: Operational empty, 14,052 lb (6 374 kg); max take-off, 26,200 lb (11 880 kg).
Armament: Five external stations for up to 5,000 lb (2 270 kg) VTO or 8,000 lb (3 630 kg) STO of ordnance, typical loads including two 30-mm cannon (on fuselage stations) plus four AIM-9L Sidewinder AAMs and two 190 Imp gal (864 l) drop tanks for combat air patrol, or two BAeD Sea Eagle anti-shipping missiles and four AIM-9L Sidewinders.
Status: First Sea Harrier (built on production tooling) flown 20 August 1978, with 57 ordered for Royal Navy and 23 (plus four Harrier T Mk 60 two-seat trainers) ordered by Indian Navy (FRS Mk 51). Mid-life update of 30 Sea Harrier FRS Mk 1s to FRS Mk 2 standard with first flight of upgraded version scheduled for February 1988.
Notes: The FRS Mk 2 version of the Sea Harrier is to be equipped with a Ferranti Blue Vixen pulse Doppler radar to provide lookdown/shootdown capability, two additional missile stations and will have provision for AIM-120 air-to-air missiles.

58

BRITISH AEROSPACE SEA HARRIER

Dimensions: Span, 25 ft 3 in (7,70 m); length, 47 ft 7 in (14,50 m); height, 12 ft 2 in (3,70 m); wing area, 201·1 sq ft (18,68 m²).

CANADAIR CL-215

Country of Origin: Canada.
Type: Multi-purpose amphibian.
Power Plant: Two 2,100 hp Pratt & Whitney R-2800-CA3 18-cylinder radial air-cooled engines.
Performance: Max cruise speed, 181 mph (291 km/h) at 10,000 ft (3 050 m); max climb (at max loaded weight), 1,000 ft/min (5,08 m/sec); range (at max cruise), 1,065 mls (1 714 km), (at long-range cruise), 1,301 mls (2 094 km).
Weights: Empty, 26,941 lb (12 220 kg); max take-off (water), 37,700 lb (17 100 kg), (land), 43,500 lb (19 731 kg).
Accommodation: Flight crew of two (water bomber) or six (SAR), and up to 26 passengers in transport configuration.
Status: First flown as prototype on 23 October 1967, and 111 sold by beginning of 1987 when production was continuing at one-and-a-half monthly.
Notes: Apart from eight supplied to Spain and two to Thailand for SAR and coastal patrol, and two supplied to Venezuela configured as passenger transports, all CL-215s so far delivered are capable of firefighting duties with two internal water tanks, two retractable probes and two drop doors. In July 1986, an engineering go-ahead was given for the development of a turboprop-powered version, the CL-215T, which is expected to fly in May 1988. The CL-215T is to be powered by two Pratt & Whitney Canada PW100/47 turboprops of 2,000 shp, and proposals exist for retrofit kits to modify existing piston-engined CL-215s to CL-215T standard. Subject to customer requirements, Canadair will offer the CL-215T with a large cargo door, underwing hardpoints, a searchlight and an autopilot.

CANADAIR CL-215

Dimensions: Span, 93 ft 10 in (28,60 m); length, 65 ft 0½ in (19,82 m); height (on land), 29 ft 5½ in (8,98 m); wing area, 1,080 sq ft (100,33 m²).

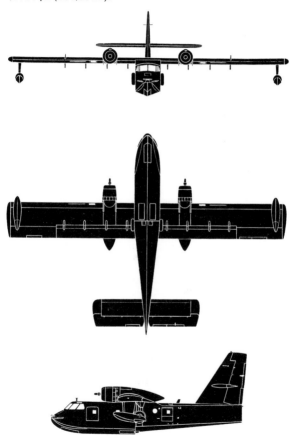

CANADAIR CHALLENGER 601-3A

Country of Origin: Canada.

Type: Light corporate transport.

Power Plant: Two 9,140 lb st (4146 kgp) General Electric CF34-3A turbofans.

Performance: Max cruise speed, 529 mph (815 km/h), or Mach = 0·8; normal cruise, 509 mph (819 km/h), or Mach = 0·77; range cruise, 488 mph (786 km/h), or Mach = 0·74; operational ceiling, 41,000 ft (12 500 m); range (five passengers and IFR reserves), 3,947 mls (6 352 km).

Weights: Manufacturer's empty, 24,685 lb (11 197 kg); max take-off, 43,100 lb (19 550 kg).

Accommodation: Flight crew of two with customer-specified main cabin arrangements for up to 19 passengers.

Status: Prototype Challenger 601 flown on 10 April 1982, and the first 601-3A entering flight test on 28 September 1986. One hundred and thirty-six Challengers (including 81 Challenger 600s) delivered by October 1986, when production was continuing at one aircraft monthly. Challenger 601-3A expected to achieve US and Canadian certification in April 1987, with customer deliveries commencing shortly afterwards.

Notes: The Challenger 601-3A is the latest version of the Challenger 601 which is the intercontinental-range derivative of the transcontinental Challenger 600. This last-mentioned variant differs primarily in having 7,500 lb st (3 402 kgp) Avco Lycoming ALF 502L turbofans. Production of the Challenger 600 was terminated mid-1983. The Challenger 601-3A offers improved hot weather performance and a fully integrated digital cockpit as standard equipment. Its CF34-3A engines produce full rated power at higher ambient temperature. A stretched version, the 601RJ, was under study at the beginning of 1987.

CANADAIR CHALLENGER 601-3A

Dimensions: Span, 64 ft 4 in (19,61 m); length, 68 ft 5 in (20,85 m); height, 20 ft 8 in (6,30 m); wing area, 450 sq ft (41,82 m²).

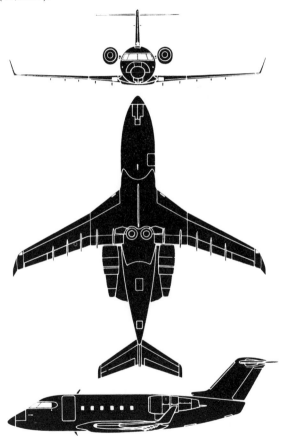

CASA C-101 DD AVIOJET

Country of Origin: Spain.

Type: Tandem two-seat basic/advanced trainer and light tactical support aircraft.

Power Plant: One 4,700 lb st (2 130 kg) Garrett TFE731-5-1J turbofan.

Performance: Max speed, 518 mph (834 km/h) at 15,000 ft (4 570 m), 500 mph (805 km/h) at sea level; max initial climb, 6,100 ft/min (30,99 m/sec); time to 25,000 ft (7 620 m), 6·5 min; tactical radius (interdiction with cannon and four 551-lb/250-kg bombs, and 7% reserves), 322 mls (519 km) LO-LO-LO; ferry range (30 min reserves), 2,303 mls (3 706 km).

Weights: Loaded (training mission), 10,075 lb (4 570 kg); max take-off, 13,889 lb (6 300 kg).

Armament: One 30-mm cannon in ventral pod and up to 4,000 lb (1 815 kg) of ordnance on six wing stations.

Status: The C-101 DD commenced flight testing on 20 May 1985. First C-101 flown on 29 June 1977, and 88 (C-101 EB) delivered to Spanish Air Force, four (C-101 BB) to Honduras, and 16 (C-101 CC) were in process of delivery to Jordan at the beginning of 1987. In addition, Chile is purchasing 37 (17 C-101 BB and 20 C-101 CC) of which all but first five are being assembled by ENAER.

Notes: The C-101 DD is an enhanced version of the dual-role C-101 CC with a similar uprated engine, but additional avionics including a head-up display, weapon aiming computer, inertial attitude and heading reference system, and Doppler velocity sensor. The ENAER-assembled C-101 CC is known as the A-36 Halcón (Hawk) and is equipped to carry the BAeD Sea Eagle anti-shipping missile.

CASA C-101DD AVIOJET

Dimensions: Span, 34 ft 9⅜ in (10,60 m); length, 41 ft 0 in (12,50 m); height, 13 ft 11 in (4,25 m); wing area, 215·3 sq ft (20,00 m²).

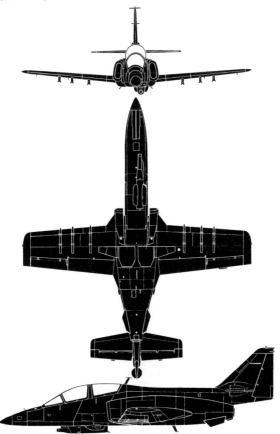

CASA C-212 SERIES 300 AVIOCAR

Country of Origin: Spain.

Type: Regional airliner and civil and military (C-212-M) utility transport.

Power Plant: Two 900 shp Garrett TPE331-1OR-513C turboprops.

Performance: Max cruise speed, 228 mph (367 km/h) at 25,000 ft (7 620 m); normal cruise, 225 mph (362 km/h) at 10,000 ft (3 050 m); max initial climb, 1,554 ft/min (7,9 m/sec); range (max payload and 45 min reserves), 305 mls (491 km), (max fuel and same reserves), 1,054 mls (1 696 km).

Weights: Empty equipped (freighter), 9,436 lb (4 280 kg); max take-off, 16,975 lb, (C-212-M), 17,637 lb (8 000 kg).

Accommodation: Flight crew of two and optional arrangements for 26 or 28 passengers four abreast, or 24 passengers three abreast.

Status: Development of the Series 300 commenced in 1983, and intended to replace Series 200 (standard version from 1979) from late 1986, when 390 of all versions had been delivered to 35 countries (including those licence-built by IPTN in Indonesia).

Notes: The Series 300 C-212 features a lengthened nose, semi-winglets on a longer-span wing, some structural modifications and upgraded avionics, an aerodynamic rear fuselage fairing (see opposite page) being available as an option in place of the rear freight doors. The military version, the C-212-M, has wing wet points for two 150 Imp gal (680 l) fuel tanks and provision for weapon-carrying pylons attached to the main undercarriage fairings.

CASA C-212 SERIES 300 AVIOCAR

Dimensions: Span, 66 ft 5¼ in (20,25 m); length, 52 ft 11⅞ in (16,15 m); height, 20 ft 8 in (6,30 m).

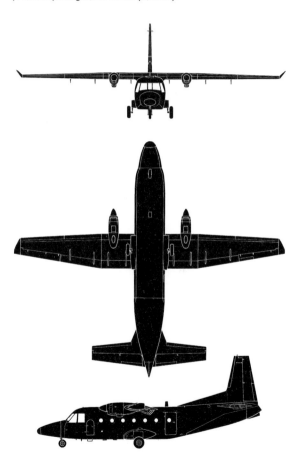

CASA-IPTN CN-235

Country of Origin: Spain and Indonesia.

Type: Regional commercial transport, military and civil freighter, and mixed personnel/freight transport.

Power Plant: Two 1,700 shp General Electric CT7-7A turboprops.

Performance: Max cruise speed, 281 mph (452 km/h) at 20,000 ft (6 095 m); max initial climb, 1,526 ft/min (7,75 m/sec); service ceiling, 26,600 ft (8 110 m); range (max payload and 45 min reserves), 373 mls (600 km) at 20,000 ft, (max fuel and same reserves), 2,933 mls (4 720 km).

Weights: Max take-off, 31,746 lb (14 400 kg).

Accommodation: Flight crew of two and (regional airliner) standard seating arrangements for 40 and 44 passengers, (combi) 18 passengers and two LD-3 containers, or (freighter) four LD-3 containers or two 88 by 125 in (2,23 by 3,17 m) pallets. (CN-235M) Forty-eight troops or 46 paratroops, light armed vehicle and 22 troops, or (Medevac) 24 stretchers and four medical attendants.

Status: First prototype flown (in Spain) on 11 November 1983, and second (in Indonesia) on 31 December 1983. First production aircraft flown (in Spain) on 19 August 1986, and first customer deliveries (CN-235M to Saudi Arabia) early 1987, when 113 were on order or option.

Notes: The CN-235 is being manufactured jointly by CASA in Spain and IPTN in Indonesia on a 50-50 basis without component duplication in both civil and military (CN-235M) versions. The uprated CT7-9C will be introduced from 1988.

CASA-IPTN CN-235

Dimensions: Span, 84 ft 7¾ in (25,81 m); length, 70 ft 0½ in (21,35 m); height, 26 ft 9¾ in (8,17 m); wing area, 636·17 sq ft (59,10 m²).

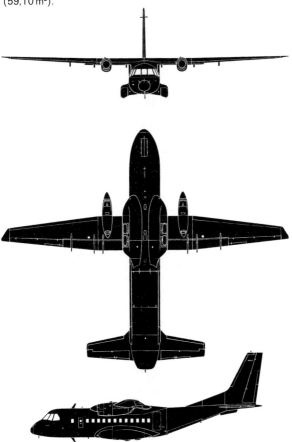

CESSNA 208B CARAVAN I

Country of Origin: USA.

Type: Light utility transport.

Power Plant: One 600 shp Pratt & Whitney Canada PT6A-114 turboprop.

Performance: Max cruising speed, 212 mph (341 km/h) at 10,000 ft (3 050 m); initial climb, 1,215 ft/min (6,17 m/sec); time to 10,000 ft (3 050 m), 9·5 min; range (with 45 min reserves), 1,284 mls (2 066 km) at 10,000 ft (3 050 m), 1,578 mls (2 539 km) at 20,000 ft (6 095 m).

Weights: Empty, 3,320 lb (1 778 kg), max take-off, 7,916 lb (3 590 kg).

Accommodation: Pilot and up to nine passengers or a useful load of 4,273 lb (1 938 kg), max payload being 3,500 lb (1 588 kg).

Status: The Model 208B was flown on 3 March 1986, with deliveries (to Federal Express) commencing in following month. Seventy on order for Federal Express with delivery rate of three monthly. Engineering prototype of Model 208 flown on 9 December 1982, with first customer delivery of the initial Model 208A (to Federal Express) following in February 1985.

Notes: A stretched version of the Model 208A (see 1986 edition), the Model 208B has been developed specifically for Federal Express (which has placed orders and taken options on a total of 200 Caravan Is). As used by FedEx, both Models 208A and 208B have windowless freight compartments and are fitted with cargo panniers (as illustrated), but Caravan Is supplied to other customers have cabin windows (as illustrated in the 1986 edition) and two- and three-abreast passenger seating. A military derivative is designated U-27A.

CESSNA 208B CARAVAN I

Dimensions: Span, 52 ft $1\frac{1}{4}$ in (15,88 m); length, 41 ft 7 in (12,67 m); height, 14 ft $2\frac{1}{2}$ in (4,33 m); wing area, 279·4 sq ft (25,96 m²).

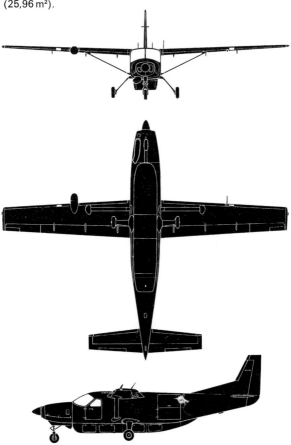

CHICHESTER-MILES LEOPARD

Country of Origin: United Kingdom.
Type: Four-seat light business aircraft.
Power Plant: Two 300 lb st (136 kgp) Noel Penny NPT 301–3 or (Series) 750 lb st (340 kgp) NPT 754 turbofans.
Performance: (Manufacturer's estimates: prototype) Max cruise speed, 406 mph (654 km/h) at 30,000 ft (9 150 m); max initial climb, 2,350 ft/min (11,940 m/sec); range (no reserves), 810 mls (1 300 km). (Series) Max cruise speed, 500 mph (805 km/h) at 45,000 ft (13 715 m); max initial climb, 4,500 ft/min (22,80 m/sec); range (no reserves), 2,360 mls (3 800 km).
Weights: (Prototype) Basic empty, 1,750 lb (794 kg); max take-off, 2,550 lb (1,156 kg). (Series) Basic empty, 1,900 lb (862 kg); max take-off, 3,750 lb (1 701 kg).
Status: Prototype was scheduled to enter flight test early in 1987.
Notes: The Leopard is an innovative light business aircraft of advanced design and construction. The small-area high aspect ratio wing combines laminar flow and supercritical technology, and dispenses with ailerons and spoilers, all roll, pitch and yaw functions being effected by an all-moving fin and differentially-actuated all-moving tailplanes. The only movable wing surfaces are the full-span trailing-edge plain flaps. The structure of the Leopard is largely of composites (primarily GRP) and the occupants are provided with semi-reclining seats, the cabin being enclosed by an upward-opening canopy hinged at the windscreen leading edge. The prototype, which is intended to prove the concept, is unpressurised and has simplified avionics compared with those planned for the series model. Detail design and prototype construction have been undertaken by Designability Limited.

CHICHESTER-MILES LEOPARD

Dimensions: Span, 23 ft 6 in (7,16 m); length, 24 ft 8 in (7,52 m); height, 6 ft 9 in (2,06 m); wing area, 62·5 sq ft (5,81 m²).

CLAUDIUS DORNIER SEASTAR

Country of Origin: Federal Germany.
Type: Light utility amphibian.
Power Plant: Two 500 shp Pratt & Whitney Canada PT6A-112 turboprops.
Performance: (Manufacturer's estimates) Max cruise speed (at 8,818 lb/4 000 kg), 210 mph (338 km/h) at 9,840 ft (3 000 m); range (with nine passengers), 621 mls (1 000 km), (with max fuel), 1,162 mls (1 870 km).
Weights: Empty, 5,291 lb (2 400 kg); max take-off, 9,259 lb (4 200 kg).
Accommodation: Flight crew of two and maximum of 12 passengers in main cabin, or (Medevac missions) five stretcher cases and two medical attendants.
Status: Initial prototype flown on 17 August 1984, with first flight of extensively revised production prototype scheduled for January 1987. Certification anticipated late 1987/early 1988, with series production expected to commence at the end of 1988.
Notes: The series version of the Seastar, developed by Claudius Dornier Seastar GmbH, retains little more than a configurational similarity to the first prototype (see 1985 edition). The glassfibre wing is completely new, the fuselage is larger, permitting three-abreast seating, and the sponsons have been enlarged to improve water stability. The hull is primarily of glassfibre and graphite/epoxy which offer high corrosion resistance, and the Seastar is suitable for operation from grass, water, ice and snow surfaces. Proposed roles include surveillance (8 hours endurance on one engine) and search and rescue, such being facilitated by ability to operate from land, water, snow or ice.

CLAUDIUS DORNIER SEASTAR

Dimensions: Span, 50 ft 10¼ in (15,50 m); length, 40 ft 7 in (12,37 m); height (on ground), 13 ft 10½ in (4,23 m); wing area, 306·6 sq ft (28,48 m²).

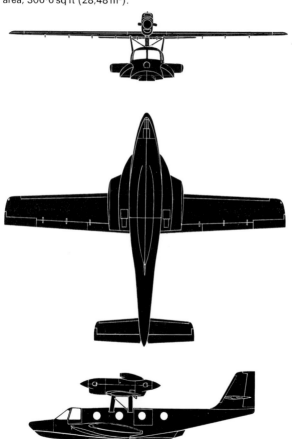

DASSAULT-BREGUET ATLANTIQUE G2 (ATL2)

Country of Origin: France.

Type: Long-range maritime patrol aircraft.

Power Plant: Two 5,665 shp Rolls-Royce/SNECMA Tyne RTy 20 Mk 21 turboprops.

Performance: Max speed, 368 mph (593 km/h) at sea level; normal cruise, 345 mph (556 km/h) at 25,000 ft (7 620 m); typical patrol speed, 196 mph (315 km/h); initial climb, 2,000 ft/min (10,1 m/sec); service ceiling, 30,000 ft (9 100 m); typical mission, 8 hrs patrol at 690 mls (1 110 km) from base at 2,000-3,000 ft (610-915 m); max range, 5,590 mls (9 000 km).

Weights: Empty equipped, 56,658 lb (25 700 kg); normal loaded weight, 97,442 lb (44 200 kg); max take-off, 101,850 lb (46 200 kg).

Accommodation: Normal flight crew of 12, comprising two pilots, flight engineer, forward observer, radio navigator, ESM/ECM/MAD operator, radar operator, tactical co-ordinator, two acoustic operators and two aft observers.

Armament: Up to eight Mk 46 homing torpedoes, nine 550-lb (250-kg) bombs or 12 depth charges, plus two AM 39 Exocet ASMs in forward weapons bay. Four wing stations with combined capacity of 6,614 lb (3 000 kg).

Status: First of two prototypes (converted from ATL1s) flown 8 May 1981, and production authorised on 24 May 1984 with initial batch of 16 aircraft. Deliveries between 1989 and 1996 to fulfil an *Aéronavale* requirement for 30–35 aircraft.

Notes: The Atlantique G2 (*Génération* 2), also referred to as the ATL2, is a modernised version of the Atlantic G1 (now referred to as the ATL1), production of which terminated in 1973 after completion of 87 series aircraft.

DASSAULT-BREGUET ATLANTIQUE G2 (ATL2)

Dimensions: Span, 122 ft 7 in (37,36 m); length, 107 ft 0$\frac{1}{4}$ in (32,62 m); height, 37 ft 1$\frac{1}{4}$ in (11,31 m); wing area, 1,295·3 sq ft (120,34 m²).

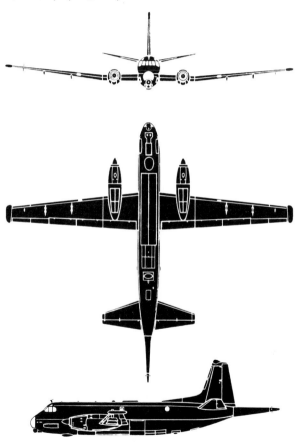

DASSAULT-BREGUET MIRAGE 2000

Country of Origin: France.
Type: Single-seat multirole, (2000N) two-seat low-altitude attack fighter or (2000B) conversion trainer.
Power Plant: One 14,460 lb st (6 500 kgp) dry and 21,385 lb st (9 700 kgp) reheat SNECMA M53-P2 turbofan.
Performance: Max speed (short endurance dash), 1,550 mph (2 495 km/h) above 36,090 ft (11 000 m), or Mach = 2·35, (continuous), 1,452 mph (2 337 km/h), or Mach = 2·2, (low-altitude without reheat and with eight 551-lb/250-kg bombs), 695 mph (1 118 km/h), or Mach = 0·912; max initial climb, 56,000 ft/min (284,5 m/sec); combat radius (intercept mission with two 374 Imp gal/1 700 l drop tanks and four AAMs), 435 mls (700 km).
Weights: (2000C) Empty, 16,534 lb (7 500 kg); max take-off, 37,480 lb (17 000 kg).
Armament: Two 30-mm DEFA 554 cannon and (air superiority) two Matra 550 Magic and two Matra Super 530D AAMs, or (close support) up to 13,890 lb (6 300 kg) of ordnance on five fuselage and four wing stations.
Status: First of seven prototypes flown 10 March 1978, with production tempo of six monthly at beginning of 1987 when orders comprised 127 (66 2000Cs, 21 2000Bs and 47 2000Ns) for France, 36 for Abu Dhabi, 20 for Egypt, 40 for Greece, 49 for India and 12 for Peru.
Notes: The Mirage 2000 is currently being manufactured in four versions: the 2000C optimised for the air superiority role, the 2000B two-seat trainer (illustrated above), the 2000R single-seat recce aircraft (for Abu Dhabi) and the 2000N low-altitude two-seat penetration aircraft (see 1985 edition). The last-mentioned is expected to enter *Armée de l'Air* service in 1988 with terrain-following and ground-mapping radar, armament being an air-to-surface nuclear missile.

DASSAULT-BREGUET MIRAGE 2000

Dimensions: Span, 29 ft 11½ in (9,13 m); length, 47 ft 1¼ in (14,36 m); height, 17 ft 0¾ in (5,20 m); wing area, 441·3 sq ft (41,000 m²).

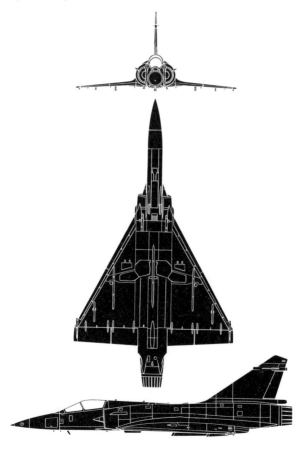

DASSAULT-BREGUET
MYSTERE-FALCON 900

Country of Origin: France.

Type: Light corporate transport.

Power Plant: Three 4,500 lb st (2 040 kgp) Garrett TFE 731-5A-1C turbofans.

Performance: Max speed, 574 mph (924 km/h) at 36,000 ft (10 975 m), or Mach = 0·87; max cruise, 554 mph (892 km/h) at 39,000 ft (11 890 m), or Mach = 0·84; long-range cruise, 495 mph (797 km/h) at 37,000 ft (11 275 m), or Mach = 0·75; max fuel range (IFR reserves), 4,548 mls (7 320 km); max payload range, 3,915 mls (6 300 km).

Weights: Operational empty, 23,400 lb (10 615 kg); max take-off, 45,500 lb (20 640 kg).

Accommodation: Flight crew of two and optional main cabin arrangements for 8–15 passengers, with maximum seating for 19 passengers.

Status: Two prototypes flown on 21 September 1984 and 30 August 1985, with first production aircraft following in March 1986, with first customer deliveries commencing late in the year. Production tempo scheduled to attain four aircraft monthly by September 1987, with 25 delivered before end of the year. Sales exceeded 50 by the beginning of 1987.

Notes: The Mystère-Falcon 900 has been derived from the Falcon 50 (see 1982 edition) with which it shares some limited component commonality, being scaled up approximately 10 per cent by comparison with the earlier aircraft and having more powerful engines.

DASSAULT-BREGUET MYSTERE-FALCON 900

Dimensions: Span, 63 ft 5 in (19,33 m); length, 66 ft 3$\frac{2}{3}$ in (20,21 m); height, 24 ft 9$\frac{1}{4}$ in (7,55 m); wing area, 527·77 sq ft (49,03 m²).

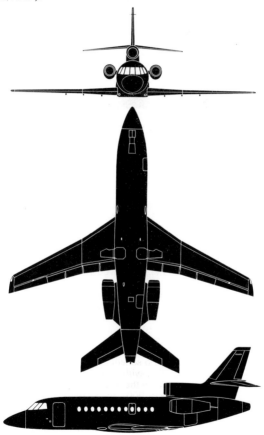

DASSAULT-BREGUET RAFALE A

Country of Origin: France.
Type: Single-seat advanced fighter technology demonstrator.
Power Plant: Two 16,000 lb st (7 258 kgp, reheat General Electric F404-GE-100 turbofans.
Performance: Max design speed, 1,320 mph (2 124 km/h) above 36,000 ft (10 975 m), or Mach = 2·0, 920 mph (1 480 km/h) at sea level, or Mach = 1·2.
Weights: Empty, 20,950 lb (9 500 kg); loaded (with two Magic and four Mica AAMs), 30,864 lb (14 000 kg); max take-off, 44,090 lb (20 000 kg).
Armament: Provision for one 30-mm DEFA 554 cannon and 12 external stores stations. Typical air defence armament comprises four medium-range Mica and two short-range Magic 2 AAMs.
Status: Single Rafale A prototype flown on 4 July 1986.
Notes: The Rafale (Squall) A is intended to demonstrate the technology (digital fly-by-wire control, relaxed stability, electronic cockpit and structural use of composites and aluminium-lithium) to be used in the proposed Rafale B intended to fulfil both *Armée de l'Air* and *Aéronavale* multi-role fighter requirements in the mid 'nineties. To be powered by two 16,535 lb st (7 500 kgp) reheat SNECMA M 88-15 engines, the Rafale B will be both smaller and lighter than the demonstration aircraft, with an equipped empty weight of 18,740 lb (8 500 kg) and a wing area of 473·63 sq ft (44,00 m²). Rafale B flight testing is expected to commence in 1990.

DASSAULT-BREGUET RAFALE A

Dimensions: Span (with wingtip missiles), 36 ft 8⅛ in (11,18 m); length, 51 ft 10 in (15,79 m); height, 16 ft 11⅞ in (5,18 m); wing area, 506 sq ft (47,00 m²).

DASSAULT-BREGUET/DORNIER
ALPHA JET NGEA

Countries of Origin: France and Federal Germany.

Type: Tandem two-seat advanced trainer and light tactical support aircraft.

Power Plant: Two 3,175 lb st (1 440 kgp) SNECMA/Turboméca Larzac 04-C20 turbofans.

Performance: Max speed (clean), 572 mph (920 km/h) or Mach = 0·86 at 32,800 ft (10 000 m), 645 mph (1 038 km/h) at sea level; max initial climb, 11,220 ft/min (57 m/sec); service ceiling, 48,000 ft (14 630 m); tactical radius (LO-LO-LO with gun pod, two 137·5 Imp gal/625 l drop tanks and underwing ordnance), 391 mls (630 km), (without drop tanks), 242 mls (390 km), (HI-LO-HI with drop tanks), 668 mls (1 075 km), (without drop tanks), 363 mls (583 km).

Weights: Empty equipped, 7,749 lb (3 515 kg); max take-off, 17,637 lb (8 000 kg).

Armament: (Tactical air support) Max of 5,510 lb (2 500 kg) of ordnance distributed between five stations.

Status: The Alpha Jet NGEA entered flight test on 9 April 1982. Four delivered to Egypt in following year by parent company, and co-production with Egyptian industry continuing at rate of two per month at beginning of 1987 against Egyptian orders for 30 of (MS1) training and 30 of (MS2) attack versions. Six of MS2 version ordered by Cameroun.

Notes: The Alpha Jet NGEA (*Nouvelle Génération Ecole-Appui*) is an improved version of the basic aircraft with a new nav/attack system and uprated engines. A proposed attack version is known as the Alpha Jet Lancier.

DASSAULT-BREGUET/DORNIER ALPHA JET NGEA

Dimensions: Span, 29 ft 11 in (9,11 m); length, 40 ft 3 in (12,29 m); height, 13 ft 9 in (4,19 m); wing area, 188 sq ft (17,50 m²).

DE HAVILLAND CANADA DASH 8–300

Country of Origin: Canada.

Type: Regional airliner and corporate transport.

Power Plant: Two 2,380 shp Pratt & Whitney Canada PW123 turboprops.

Performance: (Manufacturer's estimates) Max cruise speed, 328 mph (528 km/h) at 15,000 ft (4 575 m); max operating ceiling, 25,000 ft (7 620 m); range (50 passengers), 921 mls (1 482 km) at max cruise.

Weights: Operational empty (typical), 24,700 lb (11 204 kg); max take-off, 41,100 lb (18 643 kg).

Accommodation: Flight crew of two and standard arrangement for 50 passengers four abreast, with optional arrangement for 56 passengers.

Status: Dash 8-300 prototype (converted from Dash 8-100) scheduled to enter flight test May 1987, with first production aircraft following April–May 1988, and initial customer deliveries September 1988. Orders for the Series 100 totalled 109 (plus 36 options) by December 1986, when 23 (plus 12 options) of the Series 300 were also on order. Dash 8 production rate increasing from four to five monthly at beginning of 1987.

Notes: The Series 300 differs from the Series 100 (see 1986 edition) primarily in having a 6 ft 1 in (1,85 m) plug in the forward fuselage and offset 5 ft 2 in (1,57 m) lower and upper aft fuselage plugs. Uprated engines are installed and the galley area is repositioned from forward to aft fuselage. Six Series 100 aircraft have been ordered by the Canadian Department of National Defence as Dash 8Ms, with rough-field undercarriages, high-strength floors, long-range tanks and mission-related avionics, four being equipped as navigational trainers, and the remaining two as personnel/cargo transports. Two Dash 8s are operated by the USAF as airborne data link platforms.

DE HAVILLAND CANADA DASH 8-300

Dimensions: Span, 90 ft 0 in (27,43 m); length, 84 ft 3 in (25,68 m); height, 24 ft 7 in (7,49 m); wing area, 605 sq ft (56,20 m²).

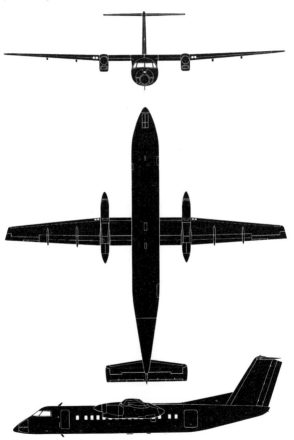

DORNIER DO 228

Country of Origin: Federal Germany.
Type: Light regional airliner and utility transport.
Power Plant: Two 715 shp Garrett AiResearch TPE 331-5 turboprops.
Performance: Max cruise speed, 268 mph (432 km/h) at 10,000 ft (3 280 m), 230 mph (370 km/h) at sea level; initial climb, 2,050 ft/min (10,4 m/sec); service ceiling, 29,600 ft (9 020 m); range (-100), 1,224 mls (1 970 km) at max range cruise, 1,075 mls (1 730 km) at max cruise, (-200), 715 mls (1 150 km) at max range cruise, 640 mls (1 030 km) at max cruise.
Weights: Operational empty (-100), 7,132 lb (3 235 kg), (-200), 7,450 lb (3 379 kg); max take-off, 12,570 lb (5 700 kg).
Accommodation: Flight crew of two and standard arrangements for (-100) 15 and (-200) 19 passengers in individual seats with central aisle.
Status: Prototype Do 228-100 flown on 28 March and -200 on 9 May 1981, and first customer delivery (A/S Norving) August 1982. A total of 108 (plus 49 on option) Do 228s (both -100s and -200s) had been ordered by beginning of December 1986, in which year production was four monthly.
Notes: The Do 228 mates a new-technology wing of super-critical section with the fuselage cross-section of the Do 128 (see 1982 edition), and two versions differing essentially in fuselage length and range capability are currently in production, the shorter-fuselage Do 228-100 and the longer-fuselage Do 228-200 (illustrated). All-cargo and corporate transport versions of the -100 are being offered. The -101 and -201 versions offer increased take-off weights. The Do 228 has been selected by India to meet that country's LTA (Light Transport Aircraft) requirement. Ten have been supplied by Dornier with 140 to be built in India by HAL.

DORNIER DO 228

Dimensions: Span, 55 ft 7 in (16,97 m); length (-100) 49 ft 3 in (15,03 m), (-200), 54 ft 3 in (16,55 m); height, 15 ft 9 in (4,86 m); wing area, 344·46 sq ft (32,00 m²).

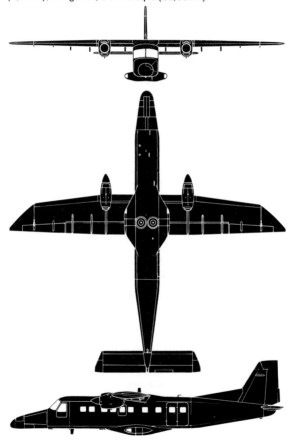

EMBRAER EMB-120 BRASILIA

Country of Origin: Brazil.
Type: Short-haul regional and corporate transport.
Power Plant: Two 1,800 shp Pratt & Whitney Canada PW118 turboprops.
Performance: Max cruise speed, 345 mph (556 km/h) at 22,000 ft (6 705 m); long-range cruise, 299 mph (482 km/h) at 25,000 ft (7 620 m); max initial climb, 2,120 ft/min (10,77 m/sec); range (30 passengers plus fuel for 115-ml/185-km diversion and 45-min hold), 1,087 mls (1 750 km) at 25,000 ft (7 620 m), (max fuel and similar reserves), 1,853 mls (2 982 km).
Weights: Typical empty equipped, 15,554 lb (7 070 kg); max take-off, 25,353 lb (11 500 kg).
Accommodation: Flight crew of two and standard arrangement for 30 passengers three abreast. Optional arrangements for 24 and 26 passengers.
Status: The first of three prototypes was flown on 27 July 1983, with first customer delivery (to Atlantic Southeast Airlines) following in August 1985. At the beginning of 1987, production tempo was in process of being raised from two to three-and-a-half aircraft monthly. Orders totalled 85 aircraft (plus 92 options) by December 1986, 24 having been scheduled for delivery in that year with 42 following during 1987.
Notes: The Brazilian Air Force has purchased two Brasilias (with two on option), and has total requirement for 24 for personnel and freight transportation. Maritime surveillance and airborne early warning versions are currently proposed for early 'nineties service. The first corporate executive version of the Brasilia was delivered during 1986, in which year the proportion of composites (mainly Kevlar, glassfibre and carbonfibre) used in the structure of the aircraft was increased to some 10 per cent of the basic equipped empty weight.

EMBRAER EMB-120 BRASILIA

Dimensions: Span, 64 ft 10¾ in (19,78 m); length, 65 ft 7 in (20,00 m); height, 20 ft 10 in (6,35 m); wing area, 424·42 sq ft (39,43 m²).

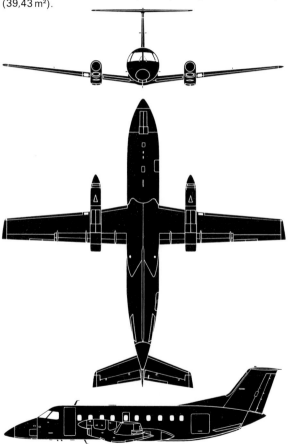

EMBRAER EMB-312 TUCANO

Country of Origin: Brazil.
Type: Tandem two-seat basic trainer.
Power Plant: One 750 shp Pratt & Whitney Canada PT6A-25C turboprop.
Performance: (At 5,622 lb/2 550 Kg) Max speed, 269 mph (433 km/h) at 10,000 ft (3 050 m); max cruise, 255 mph (411 km/h); econ cruise, 198 mph (319 km/h); max initial climb, 2,180 ft/min (11,07 m/sec); max range (internal fuel with 30 min reserves), 1,145 mls (1 844 km); ferry range (two 145 Imp gal/660 l external tanks), 2,069 mls (3 330 km).
Weights: Basic empty, 3,991 lb (1 810 kg); max take-off (aerobatics), 5,622 lb (2 550 kg), (full weapon category), 7,000 lb (3 175 kg).
Armament: (Weapons training and light strike) Up to 2,205-lb (1 000 kg) of ordnance distributed between four wing stations.
Status: First of four prototypes flown on 15 August 1980, with deliveries to Brazilian Air Force (against order for 118) commencing September 1983 and completed May 1986. Twelve delivered to Honduras. Assembly from kits being undertaken in Egypt against orders for 30 (plus options on 40) for the Egyptian Air Force and 80 (plus options on 20) for Iraqi Air Force after delivery by Embraer of 10 in fly-away condition. Thirty ordered by Venezuela with deliveries completed April 1987. Licence manufacture of more powerful version for the RAF by Shorts (see pages 184–5).
Notes: Eighty used by Brazilian Academy for basic training, with remaining aircraft used for weapons training. Two Tucanos fitted with Garrett TPE331 engines by Embraer and flown on 14 February and 28 July 1986 respectively, the first being delivered to Shorts and the second being retained for development work.

EMBRAER EMB-312 TUCANO

Dimensions: Span, 36 ft $6\frac{1}{2}$ in (11,14 m); length, 32 ft $4\frac{1}{4}$ in (9,86 m); height, 11 ft $7\frac{7}{8}$ in (3,40 m); wing area, 208·82 sq ft (19,40 m²).

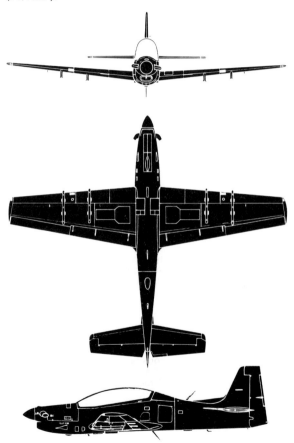

ENAER T-35TX AUCAN

Country of Origin: Chile.
Type: Tandem two-seat primary/basic trainer.
Power Plant: One 360 shp Allison 250B-17 turboprop.
Performance: Max speed, 228 mph (367 km/h) at sea level; max cruise, 214 mph (345 km/h) at sea level; max climb rate, 2,205 ft/min (11,20 m/sec); service ceiling, 24,850 ft (7 575 m).
Weights: Empty, 2,310 lb (1 048 kg); max take-off, 3,007 lb (1 364 kg).
Armament: (Training and light attack) Two 250-lb (113,4-kg) bombs, two 12,7-mm machine gun pods, or two pods each containing seven 68-mm rockets.
Status: Prototype (converted from the fourth prototype T-35 Pillán) first flown on 14 February 1986. Forty to be supplied to the Chilean Air Force with deliveries commencing 1988.
Notes: The Aucan is a turboprop-powered derivative of the piston-engined T-35 Pillán (see 1986 edition) which is currently being manufactured by ENAER (Empresa Nacional de Aeronáutica) for the Chilian and Spanish air forces, those for the latter air arm being assembled by CASA from ENAER-manufactured kits. The airframe of the Aucan is fundamentally similar to that of the Pillán, apart from some local structural strengthening, and this trainer has been developed by ENAER in collaboration with the Piper Aircraft Corporation (which was responsible for design) and the Allison Gas Turbine Division of General Motors. It is to be offered with similar avionics kits to those currently being installed in the T-35A and T-35B (for IFR instruction) versions of the Pillán. Like the Pillán, the Aucan embodies a number of standard components for the Piper PA-28, PA-31 and PA-32 series light aircraft which are supplied to ENAER as kits.

ENAER T-35TX AUCAN

Dimensions: Span, 28 ft 11 in (8,81 m); length, 27 ft 2⅓ in (8,29 m); height, 7 ft 8⅛ in (7,70 m); wing area, 147 sq ft (13,64 m²).

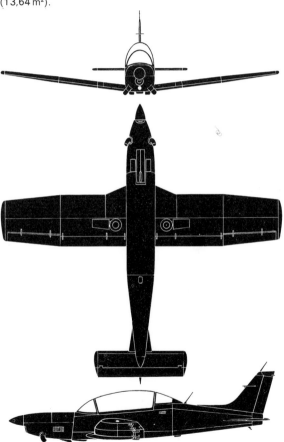

FMA IA 63 PAMPA

Country of Origin: Argentina.

Type: Tandem two-seat basic/advanced trainer.

Power Plant: One 3,500 lb st (1 588 kgp) Garrett TFE371-2-2N turbofan.

Performance: Max speed, 509 mph (819 km/h) at 22,965 ft (7 000 m), 460 mph (740 km/h) at sea level; max cruise, 464 mph (747 km/h) at 13,125 ft (4 000 m); max initial climb, 5,315 ft/min (27 m/sec); service ceiling, 42,325 ft (12 900 m); range (clean), 930 mls (1 500 km) at 345 mph (560 km/h) at 13,125 ft (4 000 m); tactical radius (attack with 2,205 lb/1 000 kg external load), 224 mls (360 km) HI-LO-HI with 5 min over target and 30 min reserves.

Weights: Empty, 5,791 lb (2 627 kg); normal loaded, 8,377 lb (3 800 kg); max take-off, 11,022 lb (5 000 kg).

Armament: (Training or light attack) One 30-mm cannon pod on fuselage centreline and up to 2,557 lb (1 160 kg) ordnance distributed between four wing stations.

Status: Three prototypes flown on 6 October 1984, 7 August 1985 and 25 March 1986. Current planning calls for initial batch of 12 aircraft for service from 1988, and total requirement of 64 aircraft.

Notes: The Pampa has been developed by Dornier of Federal Germany which continues to provide assistance to the Fabrica Militar de Aviones (FMA). The third prototype differs from its predecessors in having armament provisions and Stencel rather than Martin-Baker ejection seats. A version powered by a 4,300 lb st (1 950 kgp) TFE731-5) is proposed as the standard series model and a shipboard version was under consideration at the beginning of 1987.

FMA IA 63 PAMPA

Dimensions: Span, 31 ft 9½ in (9,69 m); length, 35 ft 10¼ in (10,93 m); height, 14 ft 0¾ in (4,29 m); wing area, 168·24 sq ft (15,63 m²).

FOKKER 50

Country of Origin: Netherlands.
Type: Regional commercial transport.
Power Plant: Two 2,160 shp Pratt & Whitney (Canada) PW124 turboprops.
Performance: Max cruise speed, 320 mph (515 km/h) at 21,000 ft (6 400 m); long-range cruise, 282 mph (454 km/h) at 25,000 ft (7 620 m); range (with 50 passengers), 1,300 mls (2 090 km) at econ cruise, (max fuel and 9,010 lb/4 085 kg payload), 2,560 mls (4 120 km).
Weights: Typical operational empty, 27,850 lb (12 633 kg); standard max take-off, 43,500 lb (19 732 kg), (optional), 45,900 lb (20 820 kg).
Accommodation: Flight crew of two and standard arrangement for 50 passengers four abreast, with optional high-density arrangement for 58–60 passengers, or 46 business-class passengers.
Status: First of two prototypes flown on 28 December 1985, and first production aircraft was scheduled to enter flight test in early 1987, with customer deliveries (to Ansett) mid 1987. Orders had been placed for 39 aircraft with options on a further 11 by the end of December 1986.
Notes: The Fokker 50 is based on the F27-500 Friendship (see 1982 edition) and the two prototypes utilise F27 airframes. However, although the basic configuration of the Fokker 50 is unchanged from that of the preceding aircraft, the series model features changes or modifications to in excess of 80 per cent of the component parts. Extensive use of composites is made in the structure and new-technology engines have been adopted, these driving six-bladed propellers, and the number of windows in the passenger cabin has been increased.

FOKKER 50

Dimensions: Span, 95 ft 1¾ in (29,00 m); length, 82 ft 7¾ in (25,19 m); height, 28 ft 2½ in (8,60 m); wing area, 753·5 sq ft (70,00 m²).

FOKKER 100

Country of Origin: Netherlands.
Type: Short/medium-haul commercial transport.
Power Plant: Two 13,850 lb st (6 282 kgp) Rolls-Royce RB183-03 Tay Mk 620 turbofans.
Performance: (Estimated) Max cruise speed, 497 mph (800 km/h) at 35,000 ft (10 670 m), or Mach = 0·75; econ cruise, 475 mph (765 km/h), or Mach = 0·72; range (with 107 passengers at 92,000-lb/41 730-kg MTOW), 1,330 mls (2 140 km) at econ cruise, (at optional 95,000-lb/43 092-kg MTOW), 1,698 mls (2 733 km).
Weights: Typical operational empty, 51,260 lb (23 251 kg); standard max take-off, 92,000 lb (41 730 kg); optional max take-off, 95,000 lb (43 092 kg).
Accommodation: Flight crew of two and standard seating for 107 passengers five abreast, optional arrangements including 60 business-class and 45 economy-class seats, or 12 first-class and 80–85 economy-class seats.
Status: The first of two prototypes commenced flight test on 30 November 1986, the second having been scheduled to fly in February 1987. First customer delivery (to Swissair) to follow in November 1987. Orders for 88 aircraft (plus options on 91) had been placed by the end of December 1986. Current planning calls for a production tempo of three aircraft monthly to be attained in 1988.
Notes: While the Fokker 100 is technically a derivative of the F28 Fellowship (see 1985 edition), it makes extensive use of advanced technology, has new systems and equipment, a lengthened fuselage, aerodynamically redesigned and extended wings, and new engines. The new wings are claimed to be 30 per cent more efficient aerodynamically than those of the F28.

FOKKER 100

Dimensions: Span, 92 ft 1½ in (28,08 m); length, 115 ft 10 in (35,31 m); height, 27 ft 10½ in (8,60 m); wing area, 977·4 sq ft (90,80 m²).

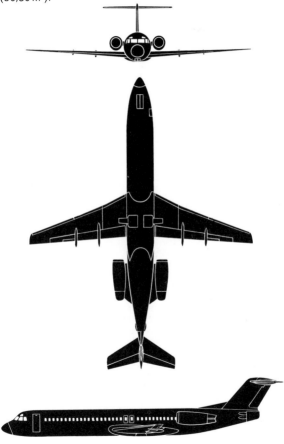

GENERAL DYNAMICS F-16 FIGHTING FALCON

Country of Origin: USA.

Type: (F-16C) Single-seat multi-role fighter and (F-16D) two-seat operational trainer.

Power Plant: One 14,800 lb st (6 713 kgp) dry and 23,830 lb st (10 809 kgp) reheat Pratt & Whitney F100-PW-200 or -220, or 16,610 lb st (7 334 kgp) dry and 27,080 lb st (12 283 kgp) reheat General Electric F110-GE-100 turbofan.

Performance: (F-16C with F100-PW-200) Max speed (short endurance dash), 1,333 mph (2 145 km/h) at 40,000 ft (12 190 m) or Mach = 2·02, (sustained), 1,247 mph (2 007 km/h) or Mach = 1·89; tactical radius (HI-LO-HI interdiction on internal fuel), 360 mls (580 km) with six 500-lb (227-kg) bombs.

Weights: (F-16C) Take-off (intercept mission with AAMs), 25,070 lb (11 372 kg); max take-off, 37,500 lb (17 010 kg).

Armament: One 20-mm M61A-1 rotary cannon and (intercept) two to six AIM-9L/M AAMs, or (interdiction) up to 12,430 lb (5 638 kg) ordnance between nine stations.

Status: First of two (YF-16) prototypes flown 20 January 1974, and first production aircraft (F-16A) flown 7 August 1978, with first F-16C being delivered 19 July 1984, and 1,604 delivered by parent company by 15 September 1986. European multination programme embraces 160 for Belgium, 70 for Denmark, 72 for Norway and 213 for Netherlands. Other purchasers include Egypt (80), Greece (40), Indonesia (12), Israel (150), South Korea (36), Pakistan (40), Singapore (8),Thailand (12), Turkey (160) and Venezuela (24). Upgraded F-16C and D have common engine bay for either F100 or F110 from 1986.

Notes: The F-16C and F-16D aircraft ordered by Turkey are to be licence-manufactured in that country with deliveries commencing in 1988.

GENERAL DYNAMICS F-16 FIGHTING FALCON

Dimensions: Span (excluding missiles), 31 ft 0 in (9,45 m); length, 47 ft 7¾ in (14,52 m); height, 16 ft 5¼ in (5,01 m); wing area, 300 sq ft (27,87 m²).

GRUMMAN E-2C HAWKEYE

Country of Origin: USA.

Type: Airborne early warning, surface surveillance and strike control aircraft.

Power Plant: Two 4,910 ehp Allison T56-A-425 or (from 1987) 5,250 ehp T56-A-427 turboprops.

Performance: (T56-A-425 engines and max take-off weight) Max speed, 372 mph (598 km/h); max cruise, 358 mph (576 km/h); initial climb, 2,515 ft/min (12,8 m/sec); service ceiling, 30,800 ft (9 390 m); time on station, 4 hrs at 200 mls (320 km) from base; ferry range, 1,604 mls (2 580 km).

Weights: Empty, 38,063 lb (17 265 kg); max take-off, 51,933 lb (23 556 kg).

Accommodation: Flight crew of two and Airborne Tactical Data System team of three.

Status: First of two E-2C prototypes flown 20 January 1971, with first production following 23 September 1972. Total of 113 ordered by US Navy, five by Egypt, four by Israel, eight by Japan and four by Singapore, with 110 built by beginning of 1987, when production planned to continue at six annually until at least 1995.

Notes: Evolved from the E-2A (56 built with 52 upgraded to E-2B standard), the E-2C differed fundamentally in replacing the "blue water" capable APS-96 radar system with APS-120 capable of target detection and tracking over land. The improved APS-138 was retrofitted from 1983, and this is to give place to APS-139 in new production E-2Cs from 1988. The extended detection-range APS-145 less susceptible to overland clutter will be retrofitted to all aircraft from 1990. From 1987, uprated T56-A-427 engines are being installed and the central computer is being up-graded, with improved IFF and enhanced displays following during 1988.

GRUMMAN E-2C HAWKEYE

Dimensions: Span, 80 ft 7 in (24,56 m); length, 57 ft 7 in (17,55 m); height, 18 ft 4 in (5,69 m); wing area, 700 sq ft (65,03 m²).

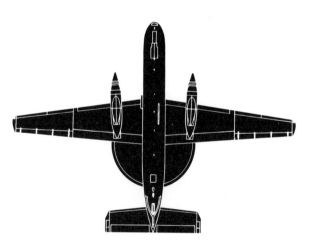

GRUMMAN F-14A (PLUS) TOMCAT

Country of Origin: USA.

Type: Two-seat shipboard multi-role fighter.

Power Plant: Two 16,610 lb st (7 334 kgp) dry and 27,080 lb st (12 283 kgp) reheat General Electric F110-GE-400 turbofans.

Performance: Max speed (with four semi-recessed Sparrow AAMs), 912 mph (1 468 km/h) at sea level or Mach = 1·2, 1,544 mph (2 485 km/h) at 40,000 ft or Mach = 2·34; combat air patrol loiter time (at 173-mile/278-km radius with two 280 US gal/1060 l drop tanks), 2·05 hrs; combat air patrol radius (with 1 hr loiter), 423 mls (680 km); intercept radius (at Mach = 1·3), 319 mls (513 km).

Weights: (Estimated) Empty, 42,000 lb (19 050 kg); max take-off, 75,000 lb (34 020 kg).

Armament: One 20-mm M61A-1 rotary cannon and (typical) four AIM-54A Phoenix, two AIM-7E/F Sparrow and two AIM-9G/H Sidewinder air-to-air missiles.

Status: First production F-14A (Plus) flown on 29 September 1986, and further 28 will be delivered (to complete procurement of 599 F-14As) before commencement of delivery of 300 similarly-powered F-14Ds of which first to be received by US Navy in March 1990.

Notes: The F-14A (Plus) version of the Tomcat differs from the basic F-14A essentially in having F110 engines in place of Pratt & Whitney TF30-P-414A which afford some 30 per cent less power. Deliveries of the F-14A (Plus) will commence in November 1987, and it is expected that a further 40 existing TF30-engined F-14As will be cycled through a re-engining programme. The F-14D will have similar F110 engines and upgraded avionics, including a new digital radar and much improved electronic countermeasures capability. The more powerful engines eliminate the need for afterburning during shipboard catapult launch.

GRUMMAN F-14A (PLUS) TOMCAT

Dimensions: Span (20 deg sweep), 64 ft 1½ in (19,55 m), (68 deg sweep), 37 ft 7 in (11,45 m); length, 61 ft 11⅞ in (18,90 m); height, 16 ft 0 in (4,88 m); wing area, 565 sq ft (52,50 m²).

GULFSTREAM AEROSPACE GULFSTREAM IV

Country of Origin: USA.
Type: Corporate transport.
Power Plant: Two 12,420 lb st (5634 kgp) Rolls-Royce Tay Mk 610-8 turbofans.
Performance: Max cruise speed, 597 mph (962 km/h) at 36,000 ft (10 975 m), or Mach=0·88; long-range cruise, 528 mph (850 km/h), or Mach=0·8; initial climb, 3,816 ft/min (19,38 m/sec); max operating altitude, 51,000 ft (15 545 m); range (crew of three and eight passengers), 4,950 mls (7 968 km).
Weights: Manufacturer's empty, 35,200 lb (15 967 kg); max take-off, 71,700 lb (35 523 kg).
Accommodation: Flight crew of two or three, with standard optional arrangements for 12, 14 or 15 passengers.
Status: Prototype flown on 19 September 1985, with certification following in October 1986, at which time initial customer deliveries commenced with 10 having been scheduled for delivery by end of 1986 when 102 had been ordered, and 43 were due to be completed during 1987.
Notes: Essentially a progressive development of the Gulfstream III (see 1984 edition), the Gulfstream IV features a structurally redesigned wing, a lengthened fuselage and Tay engines in place of Speys. A military version, the Gulfstream SRA-4, was being offered at the beginning of 1987 for such missions as surveillance, reconnaissance, medical evacuation, administrative transport, priority freight, maritime patrol and ASW. Current planning calls for an increase in production tempo to four monthly by 1988, stabilising at three monthly in the following year. Several derivative versions, including a stretched 24-seat airliner, were under consideration at the beginning of 1987.

GULFSTREAM AEROSPACE GULFSTREAM IV

Dimensions: Span, 77 ft 10 in (23,72 m); length, 88 ft 4 in (26,90 m); height, 24 ft 10 in (7,60 m); wing area, 950·4 sq ft (88,30 m²).

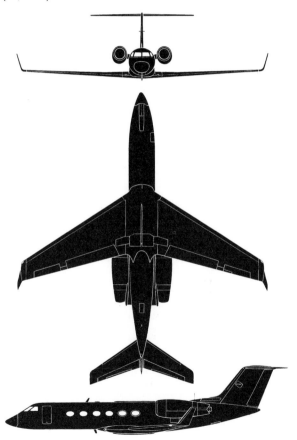

HARBIN Y-12-2

Country of Origin: China.
Type: Light STOL general-purpose transport.
Power Plant: Two 620 shp Pratt & Whitney Canada PT6A-27 turboprops.
Performance: Max cruise speed, 204 mph (328 km/h) 9,840 ft (3 000 m); econ cruise, 143 mph (230 km/h) at 9,840 ft (3 000 m); max initial climb, 1,732 ft/min (8,8 m/sec); range (with max fuel and 1,762-lb/800-kg payload with 45 min reserves), 895 mls (1 440 km).
Weights: Empty, 6,256 lb (2 838 kg); operational, 7,608 lb (2 997 kg); max take-off, 11,684 lb (5 300 kg).
Accommodation: Flight crew of two with three-abreast seating in main cabin for up to 17 passengers. Alternative arrangements for aeromedical and all-cargo versions.
Status: The first of two prototypes (Y-12-1) flown on 14 July 1982, and first of three test and evaluation models of the series version (Y-12-2) flown in 1983. Twenty-four built by beginning of 1987 (10 of these during 1986) and Chinese certification obtained in December 1985.
Notes: Derived from the seven-seat piston-engined Y-11 (of which 40 were built) by the Harbin Aircraft Manufacturing Corporation, the Y-12-2 is a development of the Y-12-1 which differed essentially in having 500 shp PT6A-10 engines. A new cabin interior and environmental control system for the Y-12-2 have been developed by the Hong Kong Aircraft Engineering Company (HAECO), and drawings and kits have been supplied for application to aircraft on the Harbin assembly line. The PT64A-27 turboprop is being licence-manufactured in China. Flight test support has been provided by Lockheed.

HARBIN Y-12-2

Dimensions: Span, 456 ft 10½ in (17,23 m); length, 48 ft 9 in (14,86 m); height, 17 ft 3¾ in (5,27 m); wing area, 368·88 sq ft (34,27 m²).

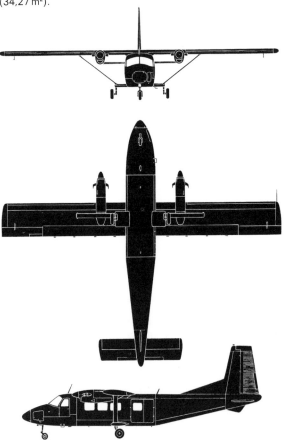

IAI LAVI

Country of Origin: Israel.

Type: Single-seat multirole fighter and two-seat conversion trainer.

Power Plant: One 13,550 lb st (6 146 kgp) military and 20,620 lb st (9 353 kgp) reheat Pratt & Whitney PW1120 turbojet.

Performance: (Estimated) Max speed (two Shafrir AAMs and 50% internal fuel), 1,188 mph (1 912 km/h) at 36,000 ft (11 000 m), or Mach = 1·8; low-altitude penetration speed (with eight 750-lb/340-kg bombs), 620 mph (998 km/h), or (two 2,000-lb/907-kg bombs), 687 mph (1 106 km/h); combat radius (air-air mission), 1,150 mls (1 850 km), (with eight 750-lb/340-kg bombs LO-LO-LO), 280 mls (450 km).

Weights: (Estimated) Operational empty, 15,305 lb (6 942 kg); basic take-off, 21,305 lb (9 664 kg); max take-off, 42,500 lb (19 278 kg).

Armament: Max of 20,000 lb (9 072 kg) of external ordnance on four fuselage, four underwing and two wingtip stations.

Status: First of two two-seat prototypes was scheduled to fly 1986/early 1987, with four single-seat prototypes to follow 1987–88. Israeli requirement for 300 (including 60 combat-capable two-seaters) with deliveries commencing late 1990.

Notes: The Lavi (Young Lion) is intended primarily for close air support and interdiction with a secondary air-air role. The third and subsequent prototypes are to be fitted with the definitive wing (with increased elevon chord) and the last three prototypes will have the complete mission-adaptive avionics system. The two-seat version is illustrated above and on opposite page.

IAI LAVI

Dimensions: Span, 28 ft 7 in (8,71 m); length, 47 ft 2½ in (14,39 m); height, 17 ft 4 in (5,28 m); wing area (including canards), 414·4 sq ft (38,50 m²).

ILYUSHIN IL-76 (CANDID)

Country of Origin: USSR.

Type: Heavy-duty medium/long-haul military and commercial freighter and troop transport.

Power Plant: Four 26,455 lb st (12 000 kgp) Soloviev D-30KP turbofans.

Performance: Max speed, 528 mph (850 km/h) at 32,810 ft (10 000 m); max cruise, 497 mph (800 km/h) at 29,500–42,650 ft (9 000–13 000 m); range cruise, 466 mph (750 km/h); initial climb, 1,772 ft/min (9,0 m/sec); range (with max payload), 1,864 mls (3 000 km) with 45 min reserves, (with 44,032-lb/20 000-kg payload), 4,040 mls (6 500 km).

Weights: Max take-off, 374,790 lb (170 000 kg).

Armament: (Military) Twin 23-mm cannon in tail barbette.

Accommodation: Normal flight crew of seven (including two freight handlers) with navigator's compartment below flight deck in glazed nose. Quick configuration changes may be made by means of modules each of which can accommodate 30 passengers in four abreast seating, litter patients and medical attendants, or cargo. Three such modules may be carried, these being loaded through the rear doors by means of overhead travelling cranes.

Status: First of four prototypes flown on 25 March 1971, with production deliveries to both Aeroflot and the Soviet Air Forces following in 1974. More than 50 in service with former and 250 with latter by beginning of 1987, when production was continuing at approximately 30 annually.

Notes: Since introduction of the basic Il-76, developed versions have included the Il-76T with additional fuel tankage, the military Il-76M (Candid-B), and the improved Il-76TD and MD. An airborne early warning derivative (see 1985 edition) is known to NATO as Mainstay, some half-dozen being in service by 1987, and a flight refuelling tanker variant has been assigned the reporting name Midas.

ILYUSHIN IL-76 (CANDID)

Dimensions: Span, 165 ft 8⅓ in (50,50 m); length, 152 ft 10¼ in (46,59 m); height, 48 ft 5⅝ in (14,76 m); wing area, 3,229·2 sq ft (300,00 m²).

KAWASAKI T-4

Country of Origin: Japan.

Type: Tandem two-seat basic trainer.

Power Plant: Two 3,660 lb st (1 660 kgp) Ishikawajima-Harima XF3-30 turbofans.

Performance: (manufacturer's estimated) Max speed, 576 mph (927 km/h) at sea level, or Mach = 0·75, 616 mph (990 km/h) at 25,000 ft (7 620 m), or Mach = 0·9; max cruise, 506 mph (815 km/h) at 30,000 ft (9 145 m); max initial climb, 10,000 ft/min (50,8 m/sec); service ceiling, 40,000 ft (12 200 m); range (internal fuel), 863 mls (1 390 km).

Weights: Empty, 8,157 lb (3 700 kg); normal loaded, 12,125 lb (5 500 kg); max take-off, 16,535 lb (7 500 kg).

Armament: (Training) One 7,6-mm machine gun pod on fuselage station and one AIM-9L Sidewinder AAM on each of two wing stations, or up to four 500-lb (227-kg) practice bombs.

Status: The first of four XT-4 prototypes was flown on 29 July 1985, and the fourth was delivered to the Defence Agency in July 1986. Series production of the T-4 is scheduled to commence during 1987, with initial deliveries to the Air Self-Defence Force commencing mid-1988, procurement being expected to total some 200 aircraft.

Notes: Intended as a replacement for the Fuji T-1, the T-4 has been developed jointly by Kawasaki (as prime contractor), Mitsubishi and Fuji. Kawasaki produces the front fuselage and is responsible for final assembly, Mitsubishi manufacturing the centre and rear fuselage, the engine air intakes and vertical tail, and Fuji contributing the wings, horizontal tail surfaces, rear fuselage and cockpit canopy. The T-4 is the first Japanese aircraft to combine a nationally-designed power plant with an indigenous airframe for 25 years.

KAWASAKI T-4

Dimensions: Span, 32 ft 6 in (9,90 m); length, 42 ft 8 in (13.00 m); height, 15 ft 1 in (4,60 m); wing area, 232·5 sq ft (21,60 m²).

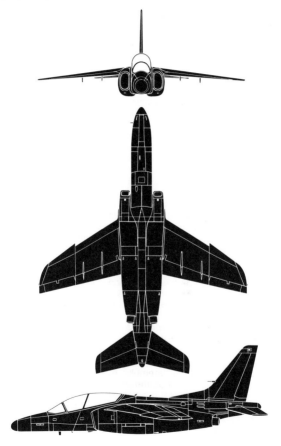

LET L-610

Country of Origin: Czechoslovakia.

Type: Short-haul regional airliner.

Power Plant: Two 1,822 shp Motorlet M 602 turboprops.

Performance: (Manufacturer's estimates) Max cruise speed, 304 mph (490 km/h) at 23,620 ft (7 200 m); long-range cruise, 253 mph (408 km/h) at 23,620 ft (7 200 m); max initial climb, 1,870 ft/min (9,5 m/sec); service ceiling, 33,630 ft (10 250 m); range (max payload and 45 min reserves), 472 mls (760 km), (max fuel), 1,336 mls (2 150 km).

Weights: (Manufacturer's estimates) Operational empty, 19,841 lb (9 00 kg); max take-off, 30,865 lb (14 000 kg).

Accommodation: Flight crew of two and standard arrangement for 40 passengers four abreast with central aisle.

Status: First of three prototypes (one static and two flying) scheduled to enter test during last quarter of 1987, with certification and initial customer deliveries in 1990.

Notes: The L-610 has been designed for short-haul operations over stage lengths of 250–375 miles (400–600 km) and is intended to complement the smaller L-410 light transport (see 1986 edition) which has been in continuous production in successive versions since 1970. Although of basically similar configuration to the earlier aircraft, the L-610 possesses no commonality with the L-410, and has been designed by the Let National Corporation in conjunction with the Czechoslovak Aircraft Research and Test Institute, Motorlet and Avia. The Soviet Union is expected to be the major customer for the L 610 as it has been for the smaller L 410. The undercarriage of the L 610 has been designed for soft field operation and for the descent rates demanded by "difficult" strips.

LET L-610

Dimensions: Span, 84 ft 0 in (25,60 m); length, 70 ft 3$\frac{1}{4}$ in (21,42 m); height, 24 ft 11$\frac{1}{2}$ in (7,61 m); wing area, 602·8 sq ft (56,00 m²).

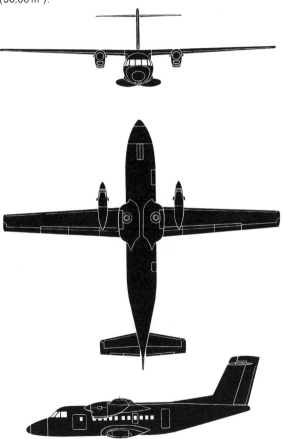

LOCKHEED C-5B GALAXY

Country of Origin: USA.

Type: Heavy strategic transport.

Power Plant: Four 41,100 lb st (18 643 kgp) General Electric TF39-GE-1C turbofans.

Performance: Max speed, 571 mph (919 km/h) at 25,000 ft (7 620 m); max cruise, 552–564 mph (888–908 km/h) at 25,000 ft (7 620 m); econ cruise, 518 mph (833 km/h); max initial climb, 1,725 ft/min (8,75 m/sec); range (with max payload), 2,728 mls (4 390 km), (max fuel and reserves), 6,850 mls (11 024 km).

Weights: Operational empty, 374,000 lb (169 643 kg); max take-off, 769,000 lb (348 820 kg).

Accommodation: Flight crew of five plus 15 seats on flight deck, 75 seats in aft troop compartment and up to 270 troops on pallet-mounted seats in cargo compartment. Up to 36 standard 463L cargo pallets, or various vehicles.

Status: First flight of C-5B took place on 10 September 1985 and first delivery to USAF followed on 8 January 1986. Total requirement for 50 aircraft of which eight delivered during 1986. Production is to peak in January 1988 at two per month with the 23rd aircraft.

Notes: Production of 81 examples of the C-5A was completed in May 1973, manufacture of the Galaxy being reinstated in 1982 with the C-5B. Although external aerodynamic configuration and internal arrangements remain unchanged between the C-5A and C-5B, the latter differs in respect of some items of equipment and incorporates from the outset various significant improvements already made on or proposed for the rewinged C-5As, all 77 of which will have passed through the rewinging programme by July 1987. Apart from a new wing, the C-5B features engines of increased thrust, state-of-the-art avionics and carbon brakes. The C-5B is claimed to incorporate some 40 improvements over C-5A.

LOCKHEED C-5B GALAXY

Dimensions: Span, 222 ft 8½ in (67,88 m); length, 247 ft 10 in (75,53 m); height, 65 ft 1½ in (19,34 m); wing area, 6,200 sq ft (575,98 m²).

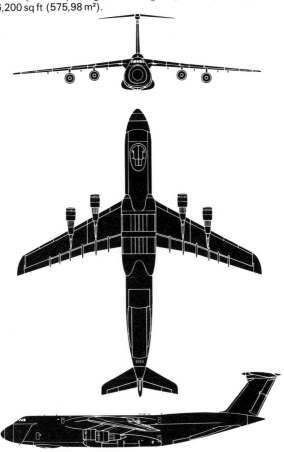

LOCKHEED L-100-30 HERCULES

Country of Origin: USA.
Type: Medium/long-range military and commercial freight transport.
Power Plant: Four 4,508 ehp Allison T56-A-15 turboprops.
Performance: Max cruise speed, 386 mph (620 km/h) at 20,000 ft (6 095 m); long-range cruise, 345 mph (556 km/h); range (max payload), 2,300 mls (3 700 km); ferry range (with 2,265 Imp gal/10 296 l of external fuel), 5,354 mls (8 617 km).
Weights: Operational empty, 79,516 lb (36 068 kg); max take-off, 155,000 lb (70 310 kg).
Accommodation: Normal flight crew of four and provision for 97 casualty litters plus medical attendants, 128 combat troops or 92 paratroops. For pure freight role up to seven cargo pallets may be loaded.
Status: A total of 1,785 Hercules (all versions) against orders for more than 1,800 had been delivered by the beginning of 1987 when production was continuing at three monthly. One hundred and five Hercules delivered have been supplied for commercial operation.
Notes: The L-100-30 and its military equivalent, the C-130H-30, are stretched versions of the basic Hercules, the C-130H. The original civil model, the L-100-20 featured a 100-in (2,54-m) fuselage stretch over the basic military model, and the L-100-30, intended for both military and civil application, embodies a further 80-in (2,03-m) stretch. Military operators of the C-130H-30 version are Algeria, Indonesia, Ecuador, Cameroun and Nigeria, and 30 of the RAF's Hercules C Mk 1s (equivalent of the C-130H) have been modified to C-130H-30 standards as Hercules C Mk 3s. Some 40 variants of the Hercules have so far been produced and this type now serves (in military and civil roles) with 56 countries.

LOCKHEED L-100-30 HERCULES

Dimensions: Span, 132 ft 7 in (40,41 m); length, 112 ft 9 in (34,37 m); height, 38 ft 3 in (11,66 m); wing area, 1,745 sq ft (162,12 m²).

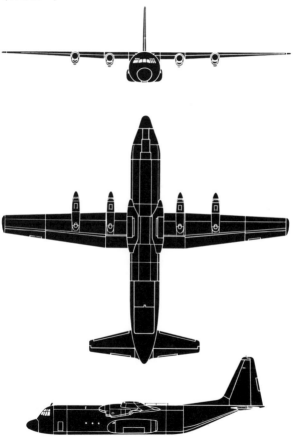

LOCKHEED P-3C ORION

Country of Origin: USA.

Type: Long-range maritime patrol aircraft.

Power Plant: Four 4,910 eshp Allison T56-A-14W turbo-props.

Performance: Max speed (at 105,000 lb/47 625 kg), 473 mph (761 km/h) at 15,000 ft (4 570 m); cruise, 397 mph (639 km/h) at 25,000 ft (7 620 m); patrol speed, 230 mph (370 km/h) at 1,500 ft (460 m); loiter endurance (all engines) at 1,500 ft (460 m), 12·3 hrs, (two engines), 17 hrs; mission radius 2,530 mls (4 075 km), (with three hours on station at 1,500 ft/460 m), 1,933 mls (3 110 km).

Weights: Empty, 61,491 lb (27 890 kg); normal loaded, 133,500 lb (60 558 kg); max overload take-off, 142,000 lb (64 410 kg).

Accommodation: Normal flight crew of 10 including five in tactical compartment.

Armament: Two Mk 101 depth bombs and four Mk 43, 44 or 46 torpedoes, or eight Mk 54 bombs in weapons bay, and provision for up to 13,713 lb (6 220 kg) of external ordnance.

Status: Prototype (YP-3C) flown 8 October 1968, with deliveries to the US Navy (of P-3C Update III) continuing at beginning of 1986 against total requirement of 287 (P-3Cs) and under licence (by Kawasaki) for Japanese Maritime Self-Defence Force against total requirement for 100 aircraft.

Notes: The P-3C followed 157 P-3As and 125 P-3Bs, and has been supplied to the RAAF (20), Iran (six as P-3Fs), the Canadian Armed Forces (18 as CP-140 Auroras) and the Netherlands (13), in addition to Japan. Deliveries of the current Update III version began in May 1984, and Update IV avionics are to be installed in 133 P-3Cs. The US Navy plans procurement of 125 P-3Ds with Update IV avionics, later engines, two-crew cockpit and elongated weapons bay for 1990–95 delivery. An AWACS version is under development.

LOCKHEED P-3C ORION

Dimensions: Span, 99 ft 8 in (30,37 m); length, 116 ft 10 in (35,61 m); height, 33 ft 8½ in (10,29 m); wing area, 1,300 sq ft (120,77 m²).

LOCKHEED (MCE) TRISTAR K MK 1

Country of Origin: United Kingdom (USA).

Type: Flight refuelling tanker and military freighter.

Power Plant: Three 50,000 lb st (22 680 kgp) Rolls-Royce RB.211-524B4 turbofans.

Performance: Max cruising speed, 599 mph (964 km/h) at 35,000 ft (10 670 m); long-range cruise (typical), 552 mph (889 km/h) or Mach = 0·83 at 33,000 ft (10 060 m); range (with max payload), 4,834 mls (7 780 km) with reserves for 345 mls (555 km) and one hour at 5,000 ft (1 525 m).

Weights: Typical empty (tanker), 242,864 lb (110 163 kg), (tanker/freighter), 244,710 lb (111 000 kg); max take-off, 540,000 lb (245 000 kg).

Accommodation: Flight crew of three with 12-seat crew rest area and (personnel transportation) 204 passengers basically 10 abreast in main cabin, with total baggage capacity of 25,080 lb (11 376 kg) in 33 containers. (KC Mk 1) One hundred and ninety-four passengers with three baggage pallets, 182 passengers with four pallets or 157 passengers with six pallets. As tanker max fuel capacity of 213,240 lb (96 726 kg).

Status: Six ex-British Airways TriStars being modified for RAF by Marshall of Cambridge (Engineering) of which first flown as K Mk 1 on 9 July 1985. Fifth and sixth aircraft to be completed as KC Mk 1 tanker/freighters during 1987, and first and second aircraft subsequently to be modified to same standard. Three ex-Pan Am aircraft to be converted as K Mk 2s.

Notes: The TriStar KC Mk 1, a military conversion of the TriStar commercial transport (see 1982 edition), will differ from the K Mk 1 in having forward freight-loading doors and a cargo handling system.

LOCKHEED (MCE) TRISTAR K MK 1

Dimensions: Span, 164 ft 6 in (50,09 m); length (excluding probe), 164 ft $2\frac{1}{2}$ in (50,05 m); height, 55 ft 4 in (16,87 m); wing area, 3,541 sq ft (329,0 m²).

McDONNELL DOUGLAS F-15E EAGLE

Country of Origin: USA.
Type: Two-seat dual-role (ground attack and air superiority) fighter.
Power Plant: Two (approx) 23,830 lb st (10 810 kgp) reheat Pratt & Whitney F100-PW-220 or (approx) 28,000 lb st (12 700 kgp) reheat General Electric F110 turbofans.
Performance: (F100–PW-220) Max speed (short-endurance dash), 1,676 mph (2 698 km/h), or Mach = 2·54, (sustained), 1,518 mph (2 443 km/h), or Mach = 2·3, at 40,000 ft (12 190 m); service ceiling, 60,000 ft (18 300 m); ferry range (with conformal fuel tanks and max external fuel), 3,570 mls (5 745 km).
Weights: Operational empty, 31,700 lb (14 379 kg); max take-off, 81,000 lb (36 741 kg).
Armament: One 20-mm M61A1 six-barrel rotary cannon and up to 23,500 lb (10 659 kg) of ordnance for the attack mission on wing and fuselage stations or on tangential carriers on conformal fuel tanks. For air superiority mission up to four each AIM-7F Sparrow and AIM-9L Sidewinder AAMs, or up to eight AIM-20 AAMs.
Status: The first F-15E entered flight test on 11 December 1986, this being the first of three prototypes, with the first production aircraft following late 1987, and deliveries to the USAF (against a requirement for 392 aircraft) commencing in 1988.
Notes: The F-15E is a dual-role development of the basic Eagle retaining the air-to-air capability of the single-seat F-15C (see 1986 edition), but having a strengthened structure, higher *g*-load manoeuvring limits and capable of day, night and adverse weather long-range deep interdiction air-to-ground missions.

McDONNELL DOUGLAS F-15E EAGLE

Dimensions: Span, 42 ft 9¾ in (13,05 m); length, 63 ft 9 in (19,43 m); height, 18 ft 5½ in (5,63 m); wing area, 608 sq ft (56,50 m²).

McDONNELL DOUGLAS F/A-18 HORNET

Country of Origin: USA.

Type: Single-seat shipboard and shore-based multi-role fighter and attack aircraft.

Power Plant: Two 10,600 lb st (4 810 kgp) dry and 15,800 lb st (7 167 kgp) reheat General Electric F404-GE-400 turbofans.

Performance: Max speed (AAMs on wingtip and fuselage stations), 1,190 mph (1 915 km/h) or Mach = 1·8 at 40,000 ft (12 150 m); initial climb (half fuel and wingtip AAMs), 60,000 ft/min (304,6 m/sec); tactical radius (combat air patrol on internal fuel), 480 mls (770 km), (with three 262 Imp gal/1 192 l external tanks), 735 mls (1 180 km).

Weights: Empty equipped, 28,000 lb (12 700 kg); loaded (air superiority mission with half fuel and four AAMs), 35,800 lb (16 240 kg); max take-off, 56,000 lb (25 400 kg).

Armament: One 20-mm M-61A-1 rotary cannon and (air-air) two AIM-7E/F Sparrow and two AIM-9G/H Sidewinder AAMs, or (attack) up to 17,000 lb (7 711 kg) of ordnance.

Status: First of 11 FSD (full-scale development) Hornets (including two TF-18A two-seaters) flown 18 November 1978. Planning at beginning of 1987 called for 1,366 Hornets for US Navy and US Marine Corps (including 153 TF-18As). First production F/A-18A flown April 1980, and first F/A-18C on 15 September 1986.

Notes: Land-based versions of the Hornet have been ordered by Australia (57 F/A-18As and 18 TF-18As), Canada (113 CF-18As and 24 CF-18Bs) and Spain (72 EF-18As and TF-18As). Separate F-18 fighter and A-18 attack versions of the Hornet were initially planned by the US Navy. Both roles were subsequently combined in a single basic version, and current planning calls for the inclusion of two Hornet squadrons in the complement of each of the large US Navy carriers. The F/A-18C embodies some new systems and has provision for recce equipment and the AIM-132 and AGM-65D missiles.

McDONNELL DOUGLAS F/A-18 HORNET

Dimensions: Span, 37 ft 6 in (11,43 m); length, 56 ft 0 in (17,07 m); height, 15 ft 4 in (4,67 m); wing area, 396 sq ft (36,79 m²).

McDONNELL DOUGLAS KC-10A EXTENDER

Country of Origin: USA.
Type: Flight refuelling tanker and military freighter.
Power Plant: Three 52,500 lb st (23 814 kgp) General Electric CF6-50C2 turbofans.
Performance: Max speed, 620 mph (988 km/h) at 33,000 ft (10 060 m); max cruise, 595 mph (957 km/h) at 31,000 ft (9 450 m); long-range cruise, 540 mph (870 km/h); typical refuelling mission, 2,200 mls (3 540 km) from base with 200,000 lb (90 720 kg) of fuel and return; max range (with 170,000 lb/77 112 kg freight), 4,370 mls (7 033 km).
Weights: Operational empty (tanker), 239,747 lb (108 749 kg), (cargo configuration), 243,973 lb (110 660 kg); max take-off, 590,000 lb (267 624 kg).
Accommodation: Flight crew of five plus provision for six seats for additional crew and four bunks for crew rest. Fourteen further seats may be provided for support personnel in the forward cabin. Alternatively, a larger area can be provided for 55 more support personnel, with necessary facilities, to increase total accommodation (including flight crew) to 80.
Status: First KC-10A was flown on 12 July 1980, with 16 ordered by the USAF by the beginning of 1983. A further 44 have been ordered under five-year contracting process for delivery through 1987. First operational KC-10A squadron was activated on 1 October 1981, and 47 had been delivered to the USAF by the beginning of 1987.
Notes: The KC-10A is a military tanker/freighter derivative of the commercial DC-10 Series 30 (see 1983 edition) with refuelling boom, boom operator's station, hose and drogue, and body fuel cells in the lower cargo compartments. When current contracts are fulfilled, 20 KC-10A Extenders will be assigned to each of the Barksdale, March and Seymour Johnson Air Force Bases.

McDONNELL DOUGLAS KC-10A EXTENDER

Dimensions: Span, 165 ft 4 in (50,42 m); length, 182 ft 0 in (55,47 m); height, 58 ft 1 in (17,70 m); wing area, 3,958 sq ft (367,7 m²).

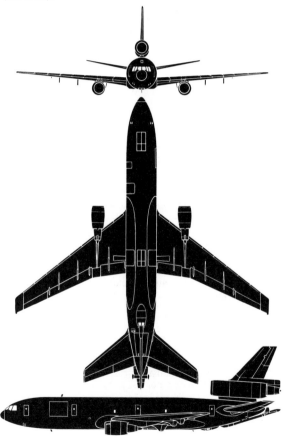

McDONNELL DOUGLAS MD-87

Country of Origin: USA.

Type: Short- to medium-haul commercial airliner.

Power Plant: Two 20,860 lb st (9462 kgp) Pratt & Whitney JT8D-217B/C turbofans.

Performance: Max cruise speed, 575 mph (925 km/h) at 27,000 ft (8230 m); econ cruise, 522 mph (840 km/h) at 33,000 ft (10060 m); range cruise, 505 mph (813 km/h) at 35,000 ft (10670 m); range (max payload), 2,144 mls (3450 km), (max fuel), 3,405 mls (5480 km).

Weights: Operational empty, 73,157 lb (33253 kg); max take-off, 140,000 lb (63500 kg).

Accommodation: Flight crew of two and max single-class seating for 115–139 passengers five abreast with optional mixed-class arrangements to suit customer requirements.

Status: The first MD-87 entered flight test on 4 December 1986, with customer deliveries (to Austrian and Finnair) to commence September 1987. Orders for all versions of the MD-80 series (including conditional orders and options) totalled 832 by December 1986, with 335 delivered and production continuing at approximately six per month.

Notes: The MD-87 is the smallest member of the MD-80 family, the fuselage being 17·4 ft (5,30 m) shorter than other airliners in the series (ie, MD-81, -82, -83 and -88) which differ primarily in weight and power plant, the MD-88 being essentially an MD-82 with an advanced cockpit. All the MD-80 family use the same wing and are available with any of the JT8D-200 series of engines. The MD-80 series is being co-produced in China, 25 MD-82s initially being partially assembled in the USA before shipment to China for completion by the Shanghai Aviation Industrial Corporation. At the beginning of 1987, McDonnell Douglas was proposing a retrofit programme for the MD-80 series with ultra high bypass (UHB) propfans.

McDONNELL DOUGLAS MD-87

Dimensions: Span, 107 ft 10 in (32,85 m); length, 130 ft 5 in (39,75 m); height, 30 ft 6 in (9,30 m); wing area, 1,270 sq ft (117,98 m²).

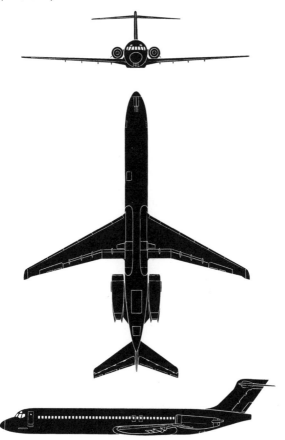

McDONNELL DOUGLAS/BAe T-45A GOSHAWK

Country of Origin: USA (United Kingdom).

Type: Tandem two-seat carrier-capable basic/advanced trainer.

Power Plant: One 5,450 lb st (2 472 kgp) Rolls-Royce Turboméca Adour 861 turbofan.

Performance: Max speed, 609 mph (980 km/h) at 8,000 ft (2 440 m), or Mach=0.85; max initial climb, 6,740 ft/min (34,24 m/sec); time to 30,000 ft (9 145 m), 6·88 min; service ceiling, 42,500 ft (12 955 m); ferry range, 1,151 mls (1 853 km), (with two 156 US gal/591 l external tanks), 1,819 mls (2 928 km).

Weights: Empty, 9,335 lb (4 234 kg); max take-off, 12,851 lb (5 829 kg).

Status: First of two prototypes of the T-45A scheduled to fly in December 1987, with second following early 1988. The US Navy has a requirement for 302 T-45As of which first three production lots (totalling 60 aircraft) were contracted for on 23 May 1986, and annual purchase of 48 is planned 1991–1995. Initial operational capability (with 12 aircraft) to be attained in September 1990.

Notes: The T-45A Goshawk is derived from the BAe Hawk (see 1985 edition) and will be part of an integrated training system (T-45TS) embodying aircraft, academics, simulators and logistics support. Seventy-six per cent of manufacture is being undertaken in the USA, and differences to the Hawk include addition of arrester hook, relocated air brakes, revised undercarriage, changes to wing movable surfaces and provision of catapult nose-tow launch assemblies.

McDONNELL DOUGLAS/BAe T-45A GOSHAWK

Dimensions: Span, 30 ft 9¾ in (9,39 m); length (including probe), 39 ft 3⅛ in (11,97 m); height, 13 ft 6⅛ in (4,12 m); wing area, 179·64 sq ft (16,69 m²).

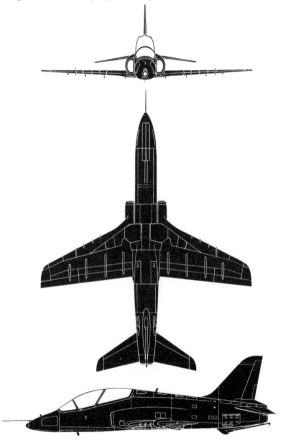

McDONNELL DOUGLAS TAV-8B HARRIER II

Countries of Origin: USA and United Kingdom.

Type: Tandem two-seat conversion trainer.

Power Plant: One 21,450 lb st (9 730 kgp) Rolls-Royce F402-RR-406 vectored-thrust turbofan.

Performance: Max speed, 667 mph (1 074 km/h) at sea level, or Mach = 0·87, 587 mph (945 km/h) at altitude, or Mach = 0·9; ferry range (with two 300 US gal/1 136 l external tanks retained), 1,647 mls (2 650 km).

Weights: Operational empty, 14,221 lb (6 451 kg); max take-off (for STO), 29,750 lb (13 495 kg).

Armament: Two twin-store wing stations for four LAU-68 rocket launchers or six Mk 76 practice bombs.

Status: First of 28 TAV-8Bs for US Marine Corps flown on 21 October 1986, with service entry scheduled for mid 1987.

Notes: The TAV-8B is a two-seat instructional derivative of the single-seat AV-8A close support aircraft which is also to serve with the RAF as the Harrier GR Mk 5 (see pages 52–53). Developed by McDonnell Douglas, with British Aerospace as sub-contractor, the TAV-8B features a new forward fuselage and canopy, and new vertical tail surfaces, but is, in other respects, similar to the AV-8A, retaining the centre and aft fuselage, wing, cockpit, avionics and power plant of the single-seater. The seats for pupil and instructor are vertically staggered, and the pupil's cockpit reproduces that of the single-seat AV-8B. The handling characteristics of the two-seater are alleged to be almost identical to those of the single-seater. The TAV-8B will replace the British-built TAV-8A Harrier in service with the US Marine Corps V/STOL training squadron, VMAT-203, at Cherry Point, North Carolina, and will be utilised for both pilot and weapon training.

McDONNELL DOUGLAS TAV-8B HARRIER II

Dimensions: Span, 30 ft 4 in (9,24 m); length, 50 ft 6 in (15,39 m); height, 13 ft 4¾ in (4,08 m); wing area, 238·4 sq ft (22,15 m²).

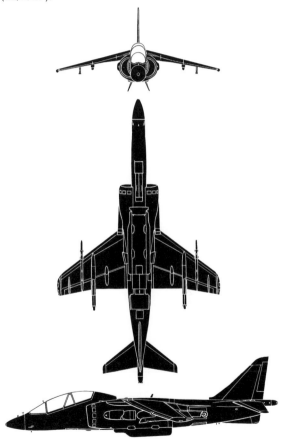

MIKOYAN MIG-23 (FLOGGER)

Country of Origin: USSR.

Type: Single-seat counterair fighter.

Power Plant: One 18,078 lb (8 200 kgp) dry and 27,500 lb st (12 475 kgp) reheat Tumansky R-29BS-300 turbojet.

Performance: Max speed (clean aircraft with 50% fuel), 1,520 mph (2 445 km/h) above 36,000 ft (11 000 m), or Mach = 2·3, 915 mph (1 472 km/h) at sea level, or Mach = 1·2; combat radius (high-altitude air-air mission with four AAMs), 530 mls (850 km), (with centreline comb tank), 700 mls (1 126 km).

Weights: Empty, 17,637 lb (8 000 kg); loaded (air-air mission with four AAMs), 34,170 lb (15 500 kg); max take-off, 44,312 lb (20 100 kg).

Armament: One twin-barrel GSh-23L cannon, up to four R-60 Aphid AAMs on twin launchers under intake ducts and up to four R-23R Apex AAMs on two wing glove and two pivoting outer wing pylons.

Status: Aerodynamic prototype (Flogger-A) flown mid-1967, with first Tumansky-engined series version (Flogger-B) entering service in 1972, with successively improved versions following in 1977 (Flogger-G) and 1985 (Flogger-K). Production continuing for attrition replacement and export at beginning of 1987 when MiG-23 remained most numerous of fighters in the Soviet inventory.

Notes: The Flogger-K version of the MiG-23 (illustrated above and on opposite page) introduces pivoting outer wing pylons, cut-out notches in the inboard wing glove leading edge and smaller ventral fin. The pivoting pylons occupy the position previously allocated to removable fixed pylons only employed with wings at minimum sweep angle and usually occupied by 253 Imp gal (1 150 l) ferry tanks. The glove notches presumably generate favourable vortices at high angles of attack.

MIKOYAN MIG-23 (FLOGGER)

Dimensions: Span (17 deg sweep), 46 ft 9 in (14,25 m), (72 deg sweep), 26 ft 9½ in (8,17 m); length (including probe), 59 ft 6½ in (18,15 m); height, 14 ft 9 in (4,50 m); wing area, 293·4 sq ft (27,26 m²).

MIKOYAN MIG-27M (FLOGGER-J)

Country of Origin: USSR.
Type: Single-seat tactical strike and close support fighter.
Power Plant: One 17,675 lb st (8 020 kgp) dry and 25,350 lb st (11 500 kgp) reheat Tumansky R-29-300 turbojet.
Performance: Max speed (clean aircraft with 50% fuel), 685 mph (1 102 km/h) at 1,000 ft (305 m), or Mach = 0·95, 1,056 mph (1 700 km/h) at 36,090 ft (11 000 m), or Mach = 1·6; combat radius (LO-LO-LO with two 1,100-lb/500-kg bombs and two AS-14 AGMs, plus GSh-23L gun pod), 242 mls (390 km); ferry range (max external fuel), 1,553 mls (2 500 km).
Weights: Empty, 23,850 lb (10 818 kg); max take-off, 39.685 lb (18 000 kg).
Armament: One 23-mm six-barrel rotary cannon and up to 6,614 lb (3 000 kg) of ordnance distributed between seven stores stations (five on fuselage and two on wing glove).
Status: Derived from the MiG-23 (see pages 140–1) as a dedicated air-ground aircraft, the MiG-27 entered service (in Flogger-D form) in 1975–76, with production continuing at beginning of 1987 in both Soviet Union and India (where licence manufacture of 165 (Flogger-J) is being undertaken.
Notes: The MiG-27 has a basically similar forward fuselage to that of the Flogger-F and -H minimum-change air-ground derivatives of the MiG-23, but is more closely tailored for subsonic ground attack operations, with additional armour, rough-field undercarriage and modified engine with fixed-geometry air intakes. The MiG-27M features lengthened nose and wing leading-edge extensions.

MIKOYAN MIG-27M (FLOGGER-J)

Dimensions: (Estimated) Span (17deg sweep), 46 ft 9 in (14,25 m), (72 deg sweep), 26 ft 9 in (8,17 m); height, 14 ft 9 in (4,50 m); wing area, 293·4 sq ft (27,26 m²).

MIKOYAN MIG-29 (FULCRUM)

Country of Origin: USSR.

Type: Single-seat counterair fighter.

Power Plant: Two 11,243 lb st (5100 kgp) dry and 18,300 lb st (8 300 kgp) reheat Tumansky R-33D turbofans.

Performance: (Estimated) Max speed (with four AAMs and half fuel), 1,518 mph (2 445 km/h) above 36,100 ft (11 000 m), or Mach = 2·3, 915 mph (1 470 km/h) at sea level, or Mach = 1·2; max initial climb, 50,000 ft/min (254 m/sec); combat radius (air-air mission with four AAMs), 415 mls (670 km), (subsonic area intercept with external fuel), 715 mls (1 150 km).

Weights: (Estimated) Operational empty, 18,000 lb (8 165 kg); max take-off, 36,000 lb (16 330 kg).

Armament: One 23-mm rotary cannon plus two R-60 Aphid or A-11 close-range AAMs and four R-23R Apex or AA-10 medium-range AAMs. Four 1,100 lb (500 kg) bombs for secondary attack mission.

Status: Reportedly first flown in prototype form in 1978, the MiG-29 attained initial operational capability with the Soviet Air Forces in 1984, and about 160–170 were expected to be in service by the beginning of 1987. Fifty (including two-seaters) were being supplied to the Indian Air Force from December 1986, and India has an option to build a further 110 under licence. First deliveries to Syria were anticipated late 1986/early 1987.

Notes: Of fundamentally similar configuration to the larger and heavier Su-27 (see pages 194–5), the MiG-29 features long-range track-while-scan radar, a pulse-Doppler look-down/shootdown weapon system, infrared search and tracking, and a digital data link.

MIKOYAN MIG-29 (FULCRUM)

Dimensions: (Estimated) Span, 37 ft 9 in (11 50 m); length (including probe), 55 ft 9 in (17 00 m); height, 14 ft 9 in (4,50 m).

MIKOYAN MIG-31 (FOXHOUND)

Country of Origin: USSR.

Type: Tandem two-seat interceptor fighter.

Power Plant: Two 30,865 lb st (14 000 kgp) reheat Tumansky turbojets.

Performance: (Estimated) Max speed, 1,520 mph (2 445 km/h) above 36,100 ft (11 000 m), or Mach = 2·3; max operational radius (with external fuel), 1,180 mls (1 900 km); ceiling, 80,000 ft (24 385 m).

Weights: (Estimated) Empty equipped, 47,000 lb (21,320 kg); normal loaded, 65,200 lb (29 575 kg); max take-off, 77,160 lb (35 000 kg).

Armament: Up to eight AA-9 semi-active radar-homing long-range AAMs (four on fuselage stations and four on wing stations), or mix of AA-9s and such short-range missiles as AA-8 Aphid.

Status: The MiG-31 is known to have been under development since the mid 'seventies and is believed to have been first deployed by a Voiska PVO air defence regiment in 1983. Some 120 were believed to be in service by the beginning of 1987, production being centred at Gorkiy.

Notes: Although the design of the MiG-31 is fundamentally based on that of the late 'sixties vintage MiG-25 (see 1984 edition), it differs from its predecessor in a number of respects, notably in having an entirely redesigned two-seat forward fuselage, pilot and weapon systems operator being seated in tandem. It possesses a lookdown/shootdown pulse-Doppler weapons system and its engines are believed to be similar to those employed by the modified MiG-25, referred to as the Ye-266M, which established a series of world altitude records.

MIKOYAN MIG-31 (FOXHOUND)

Dimensions: (Estimated) Span, 45 ft 9 in (13,94 m); length (excluding probe), 68 ft 10 in (21,00 m); height, 18 ft 6 in (5,63 m); wing area, 602·8 sq ft (56,00 m²).

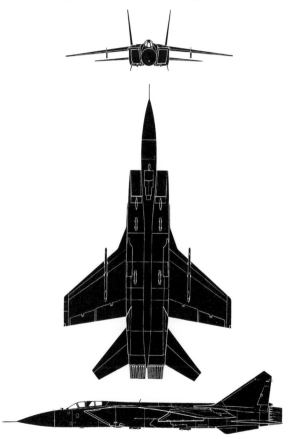

NANCHANG A-5 (FANTAN)

Country of Origin: China.

Type: Single-seat close air support and ground attack aircraft.

Power Plant: Two (A-5 III) 5,732 lb st (2 600 kgp) dry and 7,165 lb st (3 250 kgp) reheat Shenyang Wopen-6 or (A-5M) 6,614 lb st (3 000 kgp) dry and 8,267 lb st (3 750 kgp) Wopen-6A turbojets.

Performance: Max speed (A-5 III), 740 mph (1 190 km/h), or Mach = 1·12, (A-5M) 761 mph (1 225 km/h), or Mach = 1·2, at 36,000 ft (10 975 m); combat radius (A-5 III and A-5M), 248 mls (400 km) LO-LO-LO and 373 mls (600 km) HI-LO-HI with 4,410 lb (2 000 kg) external stores.

Weights: Empty (A-5 III), 14,317 lb (6 494 kg), (A-5M), 14,625 lb (6 634 kg); max take-off (A-5 III and A-5M), 26,455 lb (12 000 kg).

Armament: Two 23-mm Type 2H cannon plus up to 4,410 lb (2 000 kg) of ordinance distributed between six wing and two fuselage stations.

Status: The A-5 (Qiang-5) was first flown on 5 June 1965, and has since been manufactured in progressively improved versions for the Chinese Air Force and naval air arm, and for export (Pakistan and North Korea). The latest production version is the A-5 III (or A-5C), and the A-5M currently under development in collaboration with Aeritalia (of Italy) has uprated engines and a western nav/attack system.

Notes: The A-5 is a derivative of the Jian-6 (F-6) air defence fighter, which, in turn, is a reverse-engineered version of the Soviet MiG-19SF. The A-5 I (A-5A) and II (A-5B) featured an internal weapons bay, but the A-5 III omits this feature in favour of increased internal fuel. The Wopen-6 engine is similar to the Tumansky R-9BF-811. The principal manufacturer of the A-5 (alias Q-5) has been the Nanchang Aircraft Manufacturing Company, but currently production is being undertaken by the Hongdu Aircraft Corporation. In 1987, the British FR Group was studying adaptation of the aircraft for in-flight refuelling.

NANCHANG A-5 (FANTAN)

Dimensions: Span, 31 ft 10 in (9,70 m); length (excluding probe), 50 ft 6⅞ in (15,41 m); height, 14 ft 9½ in (4,51 m); wing area, 300·85 sq ft (27,95 m²).

NORMAN NAC 1 FREELANCE

Country of Origin: United Kingdom.
Type: Light cabin monoplane.
Power Plant: One 180 hp Avco Lycoming IO-360-A3A four-cylinder horizontally-opposed engine.
Performance: Max speed, 141 mph (227 km/h) at sea level; cruise (75% power), 136 mph (219 km/h); max initial climb, 667 ft/min (3,39 m/sec); service ceiling, 16,500 ft (5 030 m); range (at 75% power with 45 min reserves), 935 mls (1 505 km) at 8,000 ft (2 440 m); max range, 1,216 mls (1 957 km) at 10,000 ft (3 050 m).
Weights: Empty, 1,564 lb (709 kg); max take-off, 2,700 lb (1 224 kg).
Accommodation: Pilot and three passengers in side-by-side pairs of individual seats.
Status: Prototype first flown on 29 September 1984, with first production deliveries scheduled for third quarter of 1987.
Notes: Derived from the BN-3 Nymph first flown on 17 May 1969 (see 1970 edition), the Freelance features aft-folding wings and is being offered with an optional tailwheel under-carriage, both amphibious and non-amphibious floats, and with 210 hp turbocharged TO-540-C or 235 hp 0-540-J engines. The series version (illustrated on opposite page) differs from the prototype (illustrated above) primarily in having approximately 26 per cent more cabin transparency area and modest increases in cabin width and baggage compartment length. The wings may be folded within two minutes. The Freelance is intended to be suitable for a wide range of specialist tasks, including glider and banner towing.

NORMAN NAC 1 FREELANCE

Dimensions: Span, 40 ft 2½ in (12,11 m); length, 23 ft 7¾ in (7,20 m); height, 9 ft 6 in (2,90 m); wing area, 170·48 sq ft (15,84 m²).

NORMAN NAC 6 FIELDMASTER

Country of Origin: United Kingdom.
Type: Two-seat agricultural aircraft.
Power Plant: One 750 shp Pratt & Whitney Canada PT6A-34AG turboprop.
Performance: Cruising speed (at 10,000 lb/4 536 kg), 177 mph (285 km/h) at sea level, 163 mph (263 km/h) at 6,000 ft (1 830 m); max initial climb (at 10,000 lb/4 536 kg), 711 ft/min (3,61 m/sec); service ceiling, 15,000 ft (4 570 m); endurance (with one occupant and 4,486-lb/2 035-kg chemical load), 1·5 hrs; max range, 921 mls (1 482 km).
Weights: Empty equipped, 4,570 lb (2 154 kg); max take-off, 10,000 lb (4 536 kg).
Status: Prototype flown on 17 December 1981, with initial production deliveries scheduled for mid 1987, and planned monthly production rate of 1·5 aircraft from 1988.
Notes: The first agricultural aircraft designed from the outset for turboprop power, the Fieldmaster will normally be flown as a single-seater, but accommodation is provided for a second person and removable dual controls may be installed to simplify flying training and check-out procedures. The Fieldmaster is also suitable for fire-fighting duties for which it may be fitted with a fast-action water scoop. The integral titanium hopper/tank has a capacity of 520 Imp gal (2 366 l) and forms part of the primary structure, the power plant being mounted on the front of this, with the aft fuselage being attached to its rear, the wings being attached directly on each side.

NORMAN NAC 6 FIELDMASTER

Dimensions: Span, 53 ft 7 in (16,33 m); length, 36 ft 2 in (10,97 m); height, 13 ft 6 in (4,15 m); wing area, 358 sq ft (33,25 m²).

OPTICA OA-7

Country of Origin: United Kingdom.

Type: Three-seat observation aircraft.

Power Plant: One 260 hp Avco Lycoming IO-540 six-cylinder horizontally-opposed engine.

Performance: Max speed, 132 mph (213 km/h); cruise (70% power), 119 mph (191 km/h); minimum patrol speed, 81 mph (130 km/h); max initial climb, 807 ft/min (4,1 m/sec); service ceiling, 14,000 ft (4 265 m); range (at minimum patrol speed with 45 min reserves), 656 mls (1 056km).

Weights: Empty, 1,940 lb (880 kg); max take-off, 2,899 lb (1 315 kg).

Status: Prototype Optica flown (as Edgley EA7) on 14 December 1979, and first production aircraft flying on 22 August 1984. Some 30 completed by beginning of 1987, during the course of which year an annual production rate of 48 aircraft is expected to be attained.

Notes: A unique aerial surveillance aircraft, the OA-7 is being manufactured by Optica Industries and is intended primarily for pipeline and powerline inspection, traffic surveillance, aerial photography, and forestry, coastal and frontier patrol. The engine forms part of a ducted propulsor unit, the power pod being mounted downstream of a five-bladed fixed-pitch fan. The cabin configuration is intended to give the best possible all-round view.

OPTICA OA-7

Dimensions: Span, 39 ft 4 in (12,00 m); length, 26 ft 9 in (8,15 m); height, 7 ft 7 in (2,31 m); wing area, 170·5 sq ft

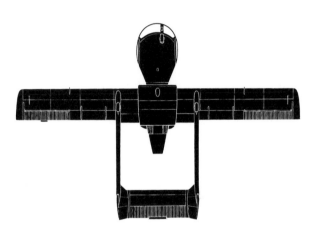

PANAVIA TORNADO F MK 3

Country of Origin: United Kingdom.
Type: Tandem two-seat air defence interceptor.
Power Plant: Two (approx) 9,000 lb st (4 082 kgp) dry and 17,000 lb st (7 711 kgp) reheat Turbo-Union RB.199-34R Mk 104 turbofans.
Performance: (Estimated) Max speed, 920 mph (1 480 km/h) or Mach = 1·2 at sea level, 1,450 mph (2 333 km/h) Or Mach = 2·2 at 40,000 ft (12 190 m); time to 30,000 ft (9 145 m), 1·7 min; operational radius (combat air patrol with two 330 Imp gal/1 500 l drop tanks and allowance for 2 hrs loiter), 350–450 mls (560–725 km); ferry range (with four 330 Imp gal/1 400 l external tanks), 2,650 mls (4 265 km).
Weights: (Estimated) Empty equipped, 31,970 lb (14 500 kg); normal loaded (four Sky Flash and four AIM-9L AAMs), 50,700 lb (30 000 kg); max, 56,000 lb (25 400 kg).
Armament: One 27-mm IWKA-Mauser cannon plus four BAe Sky Flash and four AIM-9L Sidewinder AAMs.
Status: First of three F Mk 2 prototypes flown on 27 October 1979, and first of 18 production F Mk 2s (including six F Mk 2Ts) flown 5 March 1984. Deliveries of F Mk 3s (against RAF requirement for 147) commenced in 1986. Eight ordered by Oman and 24 by Saudi Arabia.
Notes: The Tornado F Mk 3 is the definitive air defence version for the RAF of the multi-national (UK, Federal Germany and Italy) multi-role fighter (see 1978 edition). It differs from the Mk 2 in having Mk 104 engines with 14-in (36-cm) reheat pipe extensions, automatic wing sweep selection, a second inertial platform and provision for four rather than two AIM-9L Sidewinders. It was anticipated at the beginning of 1987 that the F Mk 2s would be reworked to F Mk 2A standard which will approximate to the F Mk 3, but will retain the earlier Mk 103 engines.

PANAVIA TORNADO F MK 3

Dimensions: Span (25 deg sweep), 45 ft $7\frac{1}{4}$ in (13,90 m), (68 deg sweep), 28 ft $2\frac{1}{2}$ in (8,59 m); Length, 59 ft 3 in (18,06 m); height, 18 ft $8\frac{1}{2}$ in (5,70 m); wing area, 322·9 sq ft (30,00 m²).

PARTENAVIA P86 MOSQUITO

Country of Origin: Italy.
Type: Side-by-side two-seat club and training aircraft.
Power Plant: One 75 hp Limbach L 2000 four-cylinder or Avco Lycoming O-160 two-cylinder horizontally-opposed engine.
Performance: (Manufacturer's estimates) Max speed, 109 mph (176 km/h) at sea level; cruise (70 per cent power), 97 mph (157 km/h) at 7,500 ft (2 285 m); max initial climb, 770 ft/min (3,91 m/sec); service ceiling, 13,125 ft (4 000 m); endurance, 4·2 hrs.
Weights: Empty, 727 lb (330 kg); max take-off, 1,190 lb (540 kg).
Status: First of two prototypes flown on 23 April 1986. Series production expected to commence in 1987, with approximately 80 per cent of components being manufactured by sub-contractors.
Notes: Placing emphasis on aerodynamic efficiency and structural simplicity, the P86 possesses an airframe based on a 16·4-ft (5,0-m) tubular boom of 8·66 in (22 cm) diameter to which all components are appended. The fuselage is formed of two shells of composite material, and it is anticipated that each of the first 500 aircraft will be manufactured within 350 manhours, this reducing to less than 300 manhours by the thousandth aircraft. Initial flight testing was undertaken with a 62 hp IAME KFM 112M four-cylinder four-stroke engine, but the first prototype was subsequently re-engined with the Limbach L 2000 which also powers the second prototype, and it is anticipated that both this engine and the Lycoming will be offered as customer options.

PARTENAVIA P86 MOSQUITO

Dimensions: Span, 32 ft 9¾ in (10,00 m); length, 21 ft 5½ in (6,54 m); height, 9 ft 4¼ in (2,85 m); wing area, 134·56 sq ft (12,56 m²).

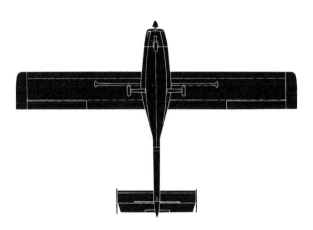

PARTENAVIA AP68TP-600 VIATOR

Country of Origin: Italy.

Type: Light utility transport.

Power Plant: Two 328 shp Allison 250-B17C turboprops.

Performance: Max cruise speed, 253 mph (407 km/h) at 12,000 ft (3 660 m); econ cruise, 196 mph (315 km/h); max initial climb, 1,930 ft/min (9,8 m/sec); service ceiling, 25,000 ft (7 620 m); range, 990 mls (1 593 km) at econ cruise at 12,000 ft (3 660 m).

Weights: Basic operational, 3,616 lb (1 640 kg); max take-off, 6,283 lb (2 850 kg).

Accommodation: Pilot and co-pilot/passenger in cockpit with up to nine passengers in main cabin, with alternative executive arrangement for six passengers, or "quick change" arrangement for four passengers and freight.

Status: The Viator prototype (originally known as the Spartacus 10RG) was flown on 29 March 1985, with customer deliveries expected to commence in 1987.

Notes: The Viator (Wayfarer) is a derivative of the Spartacus RG (see 1985 edition), which, first flown in July 1984, was a progressive development of the piston-engined P68 of 1970. The AP68TP-300 Spartacus features a fixed undercarriage, and, apart from retractable gear, the Viator introduces a 25·6-in (65-cm) fuselage stretch. The Viator is offered in commuter, freighter, combi, executive and Medivac versions, the freighter version having a 187 cu ft (5,3 m³) freight compartment and a double freight door, and the Medivac version accommodating two casualty stretchers and two medical attendants. A maritime surveillance version with 360-deg search radar and SLAR is proposed. Both Viator and Spartacus have been developed as a joint programme with Aeritalia, Partenavia forming a part of that company's General Aviation Group.

PARTENAVIA AP68TP-600 VIATOR

Dimensions: Span, 39 ft $4\frac{1}{2}$ in (12,00 m); length, 35 ft $8\frac{3}{4}$ in (10,89 m); height, 11 ft $11\frac{1}{4}$ in (3,63 m); wing area, 200·23 sq ft (18,60 m²).

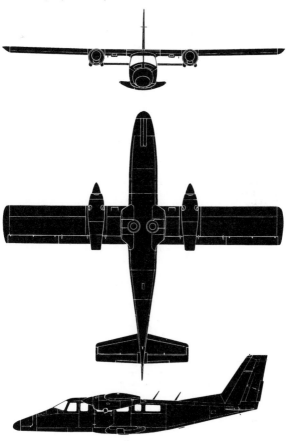

PIAGGIO P. 180 AVANTI

Country of Origin: Italy.

Type: Light corporate transport.

Power Plant: Two 800 shp Pratt & Whitney Canada PT6A-66 turboprops.

Performance: (Manufacturer's estimates) Max speed, 460 mph (740 km/h) at 27,000 ft (8 230 m); econ cruise, 368 mph (593 km/h); max initial climb, 3,650 ft/min (18,54 m/sec); max altitude, 41,000 ft (12 500 m); range (with four passengers and NBAA reserves), 2,415 mls (3 887 km) at econ cruise.

Weights: Empty equipped, 6,700 lb (3 040 kg); max take-off, 10,400 lb (4 717 kg).

Accommodation: Pilot and co-pilot/passenger on flight deck with standard executive main cabin configuration for seven passengers in individual seats.

Status: First of two flying prototypes entered flight test on 23 September 1986, with second having been scheduled to fly January/February 1987. Certification anticipated late 1987/early 1988, with initial customer deliveries early 1989.

Notes: The Avanti is of innovative configuration, being of so-called "three-surface" concept, a foreplane balancing an aft-located mainplane and a tailplane being retained for pitch control, this arrangement being claimed to result in significant aerodynamic benefits. The wing is of laminar flow section and high aspect ratio, and novel constructional methods are employed to provide an exceptionally smooth outer skin. The Avanti is primarily of metal construction, but composite parts include the foreplane, tail surfaces, engine nacelles, nose cone and some wing elements.

PIAGGIO P. 180 AVANTI

Dimensions: Span, 45 ft 4⅞ in (13,84 m); length, 46 ft 5⅞ in (14,17 m); height, 12 ft 9½ in (3,90 m); wing area, 169·86 sq ft (15,78 m²).

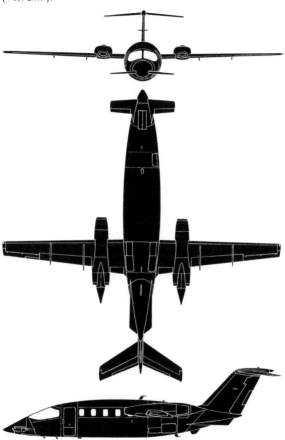

PILATUS PC-9

Country of Origin: Switzerland.

Type: Tandem two-seat basic/advanced trainer.

Power Plant: One 950 shp Pratt & Whitney Canada PT6A-62 turboprop.

Performance: Max speed, 368 mph (593 km/h) at 20,000 ft (6 100 m); max cruise, 311 mph (500 km/h) at sea level, 345 mph (556 km/h) at 20,000 ft (6 100 m); max initial climb, 4,090 ft/min (20,77 m/sec); max range (with five per cent fuel reserve plus 20 min), 690 mls (1 110 km) at 10,000 ft (3 050 m), 956 mls (1 538 km) at 20,000 ft (6 100 m).

Weights: Basic empty, 3,715 lb (1 685 kg); max take-off (aerobatic), 4,960 lb (2 250 kg), (utility), 7,055 lb (3 200 kg).

Status: First and second prototypes flown on 7 May and 20 July 1984, with first production deliveries (against an order for four from Burma) late 1985. Sixty-seven ordered by RAAF of which two to be delivered flyaway, six as kits and remainder to be built by Hawker de Havilland. Thirty ordered by Royal Saudi Air Force, with first handed over on 15 December 1986, four ordered by Angola, and 15 by an unidentified air force by beginning of 1987.

Notes: The PC-9 bears a close external resemblance to the PC-7 (see 1984 edition) of which more than 370 have been sold. It is, however, a very different aircraft, with only about 10 per cent structural commonality with the earlier trainer. The PC-9s being delivered to Saudi Arabia are supplied via British Aerospace which is responsible for the installation of cockpit instrumentation closely compatible with that of the BAe Hawk which is also being procured for the Royal Saudi Air Force. Forty-five PC-9s are to be delivered during 1987, and then 45 annually.

PILATUS PC-9

Dimensions: Span, 33 ft 5 in (10,19 m); length, 32 ft 4 in (10,17 m); height, 10 ft 8⅓ in (3,26 m); wing area, 175·3 sq ft (16,29 m²).

PROMAVIA JET SQUALUS F1300 NGT

Country of Origin: Belgium (Italy).
Type: Side-by-side two-seat primary/basic trainer.
Power Plant: One 1,330 lb st (603 kgp) Garrett TFE109-1 turbofan.
Performance: (Manufacturer's estimates) Max speed, 363 mph (584 km/h) at 14,000 ft (4 265 m); normal operating speed, 345 mph (556 km/h); initial climb, 3,200 ft/min (16,25 m/sec); service ceiling, 37,000 ft (11 280 m); ferry range (max internal fuel), 1,150 mls (1 853 km) at 20,000 ft (6 095 m).
Weights: Empty equipped, 2,650 lb (1 202 kg); max take-off, 4,415 lb (2 003 kg).
Status: The first prototype Jet Squalus was scheduled to enter flight test in early 1987, with second prototype joining the test programme late 1987.
Notes: The Jet Squalus (Shark) has been designed by Stelio Frati of General Avia in Italy and developed as a joint venture with Promavia SA of Belgium in which country it is proposed that series manufacture be undertaken (by Sonaca SA). The second prototype will have a TFE109 engine uprated to 1,500 lb st (680 kgp) and underwing hardpoints increased from two to four to provide 1,323 lb (600 kg) external load capacity for light weapons training. Under an agreement with Rockwell International, the Jet Squalus is being offered to the USAF as a T-37 successor. Certification is anticipated in Italy late 1987, with initiation of series production in Belgium commencing mid-1988.

PROMAVIA JET SQUALUS F1300 NGT

Dimensions: Span, 29 ft 7⅞ in (9,04 m); length, 30 ft 0⅔ in (9,16 m); height, 11 ft 9¾ in (3,60 m); wing area, 146·18 sq ft (13,58 m²).

PZL M-26 ISKIERKA

Country of Origin: Poland.
Type: Tandem two-seat primary/basic trainer.
Power Plant: One 205 hp PZL (Franklin) F6A350C1 six-cylinder horizontally-opposed engine.
Performance: (Manufacturer's estimates) Max speed, 168 mph (270 km/h) at sea level; max cruise, 165 mph (265 km/h) at 4,920 ft (1 500 m); max initial climb, 846 ft/min (4,30 m/sec); range (with max fuel and 30 min reserves), 584 mls (940 km).
Weights: Operational empty, 1,984 lb (900 kg); max take-off, 2,756 lb (1 250 kg).
Status: First prototype flown on 18 July 1986. No production plans announced by the beginning of 1987.
Notes: The Iskierka (Little Spark) has been developed by the WSK-PZL Mielec and embodies some components of the M-20 Mewa (Gull), a Polish version of the Piper PA-34 Seneca II, in the wings, tail assembly, undercarriage, electrical and power systems. Designed to FAR Pt 23, the Iskierka is intended primarily for civil pilot training and for pilot selection for military training in which roles it is proposed as a successor to the PZL-110 Koliber (Humming Bird), a version of the Socata Rallye 100 ST built by WSK-PZL Warszawa-Okecie. The Iskierka was originally designed for the training of Polish Air Force students up to conversion to the pure jet TS-11 Iskra (Spark) for the basic instructional stage, a task for which the competitive and more powerful PZL-130 Orlik (Eaglet) has been selected by the Polish Air Force. A more powerful version of the Iskierka, the M-26-01, is proposed with a 300 hp Avco Lycoming engine.

PZL M-26 ISKIERKA

Dimensions: Span, 31 ft 5⅞ in (9,60 m); length, 27 ft 2 in (8,28 m); height, 9 ft 8½ in (2,96 m).

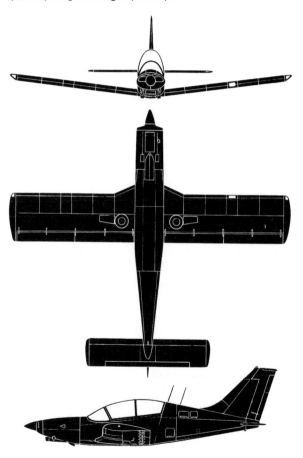

PZL-130T ORLIK-TURBO

Country of Origin: Poland.
Type: Tandem two-seat primary/basic trainer.
Power Plant: One 550 shp Pratt & Whitney Canada PT6A-25A turboprop.
Performance: (Manufacturer's estimates) Max speed, 310 mph (499 km/h) at 15,000 ft (4 570 m); max initial climb, 2,953 ft/min (15,0 m/sec; time to 20,000 ft (6 095 m), 9·7 min; max range, 1,243 mls (2 000 km).
Weights: Empty, 2,205 lb (1 000 kg); take-off (aerobatic), 3,197 lb (1 450 kg).
Armament: (Training) Four wing stations for up to 1,410 lb (640 kg) of rocket or gun pods.
Status: The prototype Orlik-Turbo (modified from an Orlik airframe by Airtech Canada) was first flown in August 1986.
Notes: The Orlik-Turbo is proposed as the standard export version of the piston-engined PZL-130 Orlik (see 1986 edition) which has been developed for the Polish Air Force. The first of three prototypes of the Orlik (Eaglet) was flown on 12 October 1984, and a pre-series of 10 aircraft was being built in 1986. The series model for Polish domestic use is expected to be powered by the PZL K-8AA, a derivative of the 330 hp Vedeneev M-14PM nine-cylinder radial engine powering the prototypes. The Orlik and Orlik-Turbo feature a low aspect ratio wing which permits simulation of the roll yaw characteristics and low speed sink rates typical of high-performance combat aircraft.

PZL-130T ORLIK-TURBO

Dimensions: Span, 26 ft 3 in (8 00 m); length, 28 ft 5¾ in (8,68 m); height, 13 ft 1½ in (4,00 m); wing area, 132·18 sq ft (12,28 m²).

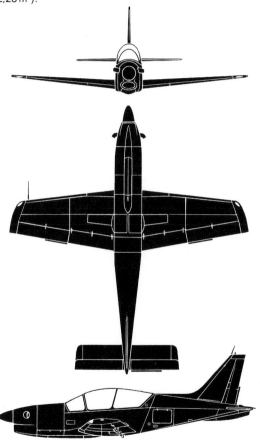

RHEIN-FLUGZEUGBAU FANTRAINER

Country of Origin: Federal Germany.
Type: Tandem two-seat primary/basic trainer.
Power Plant: One (Fantrainer 400) 420 shp Allison 250-C20B, or (Fantrainer 600) 650 shp Allison 250-C30 turbo-shaft driving a five-bladed ducted fan.
Performance: (Fantrainer 400) Max speed, 230 mph (370 km/h) at 10,000 ft (3 050 m); max initial climb, 1,550 ft/min (7,5 m/sec); max range, 1,094 mls (1 760 km). (Fantrainer 600) Max speed, 259 mph (417 km/h) at 18,000 ft (5 485 m); max initial climb, 3,000 ft/min (15 m/sec); max range, 864 mls (1 390 km).
Weights: (Fantrainer 400) Empty, 2,456 lb (1 114 kg); max take-off, 3,968 lb (1 800 kg). (Fantrainer 600) Empty, 2,557 lb (1 160 kg); max take-off, 5,071 lb (2 300 kg).
Status: First of two prototypes flown 27 October 1977, and first production aircraft (Fantrainer 600) flown on 12 August 1984. The Royal Thai Air Force has ordered 30 Fantrainer 400s and 17 (with option on 26 more) Fantrainer 600s of which two flyaway and remainder assembled at the RTAF's Don Muang base.
Notes: First six Thai-assembled aircraft have GRP (glass reinforced plastic) wings with remainder to have Thai-manufactured metal wings. The Fantrainer 600 has been modified in Thailand to carry a pod-mounted 20-mm cannon as potential replacement for Cessna O-1 and Rockwell OV-10 in RTAF service. A modified version of the Fantrainer with a different fan, revised cockpit instrumentation and other more minor changes is to be subjected to a new *Luftwaffe* evaluation during 1987 as a potential successor to the Piaggio P.149D trainer, with a possible initial *Luftwaffe* requirement for 20 aircraft.

RHEIN-FLUGZEUGBAU FANTRAINER

Dimensions: Span, 31 ft 10 in (9,70 m); length, 30 ft 3½ in (9,23 m); height, 9 ft 10 in (3,00 m); wing area, 149·6 sq ft (13,90 m²).

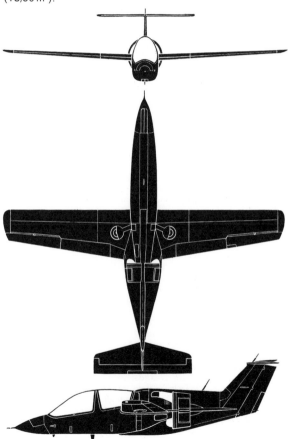

ROCKWELL B-1B

Country of Origin: USA.
Type: Strategic bomber and cruise missile carrier.
Power Plant: Four 30,780 lb st (13 960 kgp) General Electric F101-GE-102 turbofans.
Performance: Max speed (without external load), 795 mph (1 280 km/h) or Mach=1·25 above 36,000 ft (10 975 m); low-level penetration speed, 610 mph (980 km/h) or Mach=0·8 at 200 ft (60 m); unrefuelled range (approx), 7,500 mls (12 070 km).
Weights: Empty, 184,300 lb (83 500 kg); empty equipped, 192,000 lb (87 090 kg); design flight, 395,000 lb (179 172 kg); max take-off, 477,000 lb (216 367 kg).
Accommodation: Flight crew of four comprising pilot, co-pilot/navigator, defensive systems operator and offensive systems operator.
Armament: Two fuselage weapons bays to carry up to 84 500-lb (227-kg) Mk 82 bombs, 24 2,000-lb (908-kg) Mk 84 bombs, 24 2,439-lb (1 106-kg) B-83 nuclear bombs, or eight AGM-86B air-launched cruise missiles plus 12 AGM-69 defence-suppression missiles. Up to 44 Mk 82 bombs or 14 720-lb (327-kg) B-61 nuclear bombs, or 14 AGM-86B missiles distributed between eight external hardpoints.
Status: First of 100 production B-1Bs flown on 18 October 1984, with initial deliveries commencing 29 June 1985. Initial operational capability was attained in October 1986, with production of four monthly by end of that year and 100th to be delivered April 1988.
Notes: An extensively revised derivative of the B-1A, the first of four prototypes of which flew on 23 December 1974, the B-1B is expected to operate primarily at high subsonic speeds at low altitudes. Apart from serving to launch cruise missiles or to deliver free-fall bombs, the B-1B can fulfil long-range sea surveillance, aerial mine-laying and other roles.

ROCKWELL B-1B

Dimensions: Span (15 degree sweep), 136 ft 8½ in (41, 67 m), (67·5 deg sweep), 78 ft 2½ in (23,84 m); length, 147 ft 0 in (44,81 m); height, 34 ft 0 in (10,36 m); wing area (approx), 1,950 sq ft (181,20 m²).

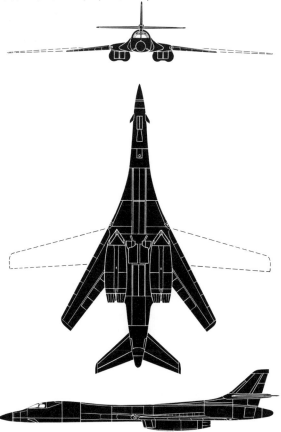

SAAB 39 GRIPEN

Country of Origin: Sweden.
Type: Single-seat multi-role fighter.
Power Plant: One (approx) 18,000 lb st (8165 kgp) reheat General Electric/Volvo Flygmotor RM 12 turbofan.
Performance: No details available for publication, but max speed is expected to range from 914 mph (1470 km/h) at sea level, or Mach=1·2, to 1,450 mph (2555 km/h) above 36,00 ft (10 975 m), or Mach=2·2.
Weights: Approx clean loaded, 17,650 lb (8 00 kg).
Armament: One 27-mm Mauser BK27 cannon. Six wing stations for ordnance (including wingtip stations) for up to four Rb 72 Sky Flash and two Rb 24 Sidewinder AAMs. Underwing stations can carry Saab-Bofors RBS 15F or other heavy anti-shipping missiles, electro-optically guided air-to-surface missiles or bombs.
Status: First of five prototypes scheduled to enter flight test late 1987. Contracts placed for 30 aircraft with options on a further 110 aircraft. First deliveries to the Swedish Air Force scheduled for 1992.
Notes: The Saab 39 Gripen (Griffon), or JAS (Jakt/Attack/Spaning—Fighter/Attack/Reconnaissance) 39, is the lightest of the new canard-configuration fighters, and the basic operational version is intended to be modified for its assigned primary mission by means of role kits, with all the hardware and software for the three alternative roles permanently carried. A tandem two-seat version, the JAS 39SK with a 1 ft 8 in (50-cm) fuselage plug for the second cockpit and all weapons systems retained, is currently proposed. The Gripen will be capable of operating from 3,280-ft (1 000-m) of highway.

SAAB 39 GRIPEN

Approximate Dimensions: Span, 26 ft 3 in (8,00 m); length, 46 ft 0 in (14,00 m).

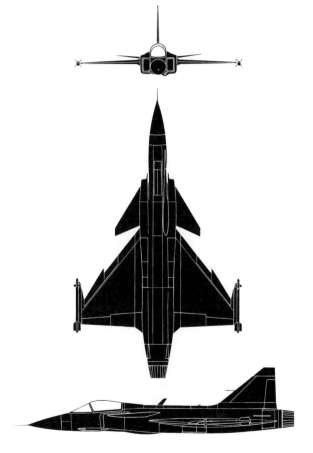

SAAB SF340

Country of Origin: Sweden.
Type: Regional commercial and corporate transport.
Power Plant: Two 1,735 shp General Electric CT7-5A2 turboprops.
Performance: Max cruising speed, 320 mph (515 km/h) at 15,000 ft (4 570 m); econ cruise, 300 mph (484 km/h) at 25,000 ft (7 620 m); max initial climb, 1,765 ft/min (8,94 m/sec); range (max payload), 904 mls (1 455 km), (max fuel), 2,470 mls (3 975 km).
Weights: Operational empty (typical), 17,215 lb (7 810 kg); max take-off, 27,275 lb (12 370 kg).
Accommodation: Flight crew of two and standard regional airline arrangement for 35 passengers three abreast. Various optional arrangements are available for the corporate transport version up to 16 passengers.
Status: First of three prototypes flown on 25 January 1983. First production aircraft flown on 5 March 1984. Firm orders for 90 placed by December 1986 of which 77 delivered by beginning of 1987 when production tempo being reduced from 40 to 30 aircraft per annum.
Notes: SF340 originally developed jointly with Fairchild of the USA, latter relinquishing partnership on 1 November 1985, and the 109th aircraft is to be the first completely built by Saab-Scania. Consideration of stretched version (approx 40 seats) at beginning of 1987, with decision anticipated during course of year.

SAAB SF340

Dimensions: Span, 70 ft 4 in (21,44 m); length, 64 ft 6 in (19,67 m); height, 22 ft 6 in (6,87 m); wing area, 450 sq ft (41,81 m²).

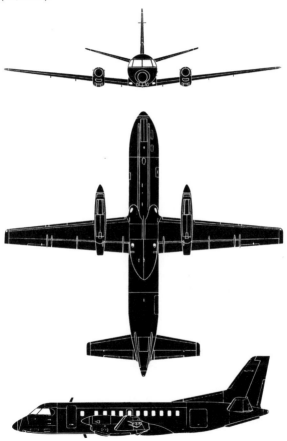

SHENYANG J-8B (F-8 II)

Country of Origin: China.
Type: Single-seat multi-role fighter.
Power Plant: Two 14,550 lb st (6 600 kgp) reheat Chengdu Wopen-13 turbojets.
Performance: Max speed, 1,452 mph (2 337 km/h) above 36,000 ft (10 975 m), or Mach = 2·2; service ceiling, 65,620 ft (20 000 m); max range (with external tanks on fuselage centreline and outboard wing stations), 1,367 mls (2 200 km).
Weights: Empty, 21,649 lb (9 820 kg); normal loaded, 31,525 lb (14 300 kg); max take-off, 39,242 lb (17 800 kg).
Armament: Two 23-mm twin-barrel cannon and (intercept mission) up to six PL-2B or PL-7 infra-red or semi-active radar homing AAMs, or (close air support) up to 8,818 lb (4 000 kg) of ordnance distributed between one fuselage and six wing stores stations.
Status: The first prototype J-8B was flown mid-1985, and production aircraft are expected to be delivered to the People's Republic of China Air Force from 1988–89.
Notes: The J-8B (also referred to by the export designation of F-8 II) is a development of the early 'seventies J 8 which was manufactured in limited numbers (see 1986 edition). It differs from the earlier model fundamentally in replacing the circular pitot air intake with lateral intakes, the new nose section permitting installation of a dual-role radar. It also possesses uprated engines. During 1986, agreement was reached with the US government for the supply of avionics system kits for installation in the J-8B, flight testing with the US equipment being expected to commence in 1991–92. The primary mission requirement is for air-air interception, including a look-down mode, and the kits are to include radar, INS navigation, air data computer, a data bus and head-up cockpit display units. Initial production J-8Bs are expected to have an alternative avionics suite.

SHENYANG J-8B (F-8 II)

Dimensions: Span, 30 ft 7⅞ in (9,34 m); length, 70 ft 10 in (21,59 m) including probe; height, 17 ft 9 in (5,41 m); wing area, 454·25 sq ft (42,20 m²).

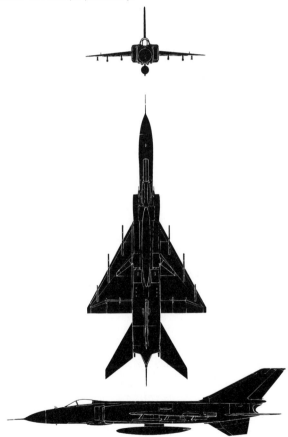

SHORTS 360 ADVANCED

Country of Origin: United Kingdom.
Type: Regional commercial transport.
Power Plant: Two 1,424 shp Pratt & Whitney Canada PT64-65AR turboprops.
Performance: Max cruising speed, 244 mph (393 km/h) at 10,000 ft (3 050 m); long range cruise, 207 mph (333 km/h) at 10,000 ft (3 050 m); range (with max payload), 259 mls (417 km), (max fuel), 992 mls (1 596 km).
Weights: Operational empty, 16,950 lb (7 688 kg); max take-off, 26,453 lb (11 999 kg).
Accommodation: Flight crew of two with standard all-passenger cabin arrangement for 36 seats three abreast, and optional "combi" (one ton of cargo and 24 passengers or all-freight (8,300 lb/3 765 kg) arrangements.
Status: Prototype flown on 1 June 1981, with first production aircraft following on 19 August 1982 and entering service (with Suburban Airlines) in the following December. The Shorts 360 Advanced was introduced in November 1985. Orders and options totalled approximately 140 aircraft at the beginning of November 1986, with about 110 delivered.
Notes: The "Advanced" version of the Shorts 360 has been upgraded with the use of the more powerful -65AR engines, new-design lightweight seats and a flight deck with digital avionics. The basic Shorts 360 is a growth version of the Shorts 330 (see 1983 edition), which continues in production in parallel. The later aircraft differs from its progenitor primarily in having a 3-ft (91-cm) cabin stretch ahead of the wing and an entirely redesigned rear fuselage and tail assembly. The fuselage stretch has permitted the insertion of two additional three-seat rows in the main cabin and has resulted in reduced aerodynamic drag by comparison with the earlier aircraft.

SHORTS 360 ADVANCED

Dimensions: Span, 74 ft 10 in (22,81 m); length, 70 ft 10 in (21,59 m); height, 23 ft 8 in (7,21 m); wing area, 454 sq ft (42,18 m²).

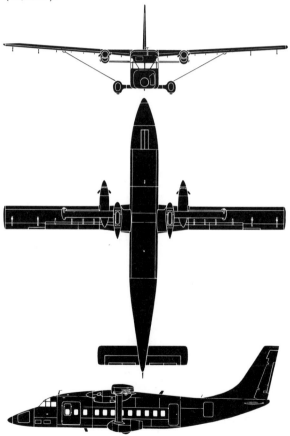

SHORTS S312 TUCANO

Country of Origin: United Kingdom (Brazil).
Type: Tandem two-seat basic trainer.
Power Plant: One 1,100 shp Garrett TPE331-12B/701A turboprop.
Performance: Max speed (at 4,850 lb/2 200 kg), 320 mph (515 km/h) at 14,000 ft (4 270 m), (at 5,732 lb/2 600 kg), 315 mph (508 km/h) at 12,500 ft (3 810 m); econ cruise, 253 mph (407 km/h) at 20,000 ft (6 100 m); max initial climb, 3,510 ft/min (17,83 m/sec); range (with 30 min reserves), 1,082 mls (1 742 km) at 25,000 ft (7 620 m), (with two 72·6 Imp gal/300 l external tanks), 2,073 mls (3 335 km).
Weights: Basic empty, 4,447 lb (2 017 kg); max take-off (aerobatic), 5,842 lb (2 650 kg), (weapons configuration), 7,220 lb (3 275 kg).
Armament: (Training and counter insurgency) Four wing stations for (typical) two 7,62-mm C-2 machine gun pods and two 250-lb (113,4-kg) bombs, paired 5-in (12,7-cm) rockets, or LM-37/7A or LM-70/7 rocket pods.
Status: Brazilian-built prototype flown on 14 February 1986, with first Shorts-built aircraft having been scheduled to commence flight test late that year. Total of 130 ordered by the RAF, with deliveries scheduled to commence early 1987. Production to attain four monthly in 1989.
Notes: The Shorts Tucano has been developed from the EMB-312 Tucano (see pages 92–3) specifically to meet RAAF requirements, embodying a new Garrett engine, structural strengthening for increased manœuvre loads and fatigue life, a new cockpit layout, a ventral air brake, etc.

SHORTS S312 TUCANO

Dimensions: Span, 37 ft 0 in (11,28 m); length, 32 ft 4¼ in (9,86 m); height, 11 ft 1⅞ in (3,40 m); wing area, 208·07 sq ft (19,33 m²).

SIAI MARCHETTI S.211

Country of Origin: Italy.
Type: Tandem two-seat basic trainer.
Power Plant: One 2,500 lb st (1 134 kgp) Pratt & Whitney Canada JT15D-4C turbofan.
Performance: Max speed, 414 mph (667 km/h) at 20,000 ft (6 095 m), 371 mph (597 km/h) at sea level; max initial climb, 3,800 ft/min (19,30 m/sec); max range (internal fuel with 30 min reserves), 1,036 mls (1 668 km); ferry range (with two 77 Imp gal/350 l external tanks), 1,543 mls (2 483 km).
Weights: Empty equipped, 3,560 lb (1 615 kg); Max take-off (clean), 5,952 lb (2 700 kg), (with external stores), 6,834 lb (3 100 kg).
Armament: (Training and light attack) Max external load of 1,320 lb (600 kg) distributed between four wing stations.
Status: First of three prototypes flown on 10 April 1981, and first production examples (for Singapore) flown on 4 October 1984, with deliveries commencing in the following year. Thirty ordered by Singapore (of which 20 being supplied as partial kits) with deliveries continuing at beginning of 1987. Four ordered by Haiti.
Notes: Intended to compete realistically in operating cost with current turboprop-powered basic trainers, the S.211 can be used for a proportion of the primary instructional phase. It possesses the lowest airframe weight of any current pure jet trainer other than the Jet Squalus (see pages 166–7), and versions with more advanced avionics and an uprated engine are being offered. These, equipped with an advanced light-weight head-up dis- and navigation computer, combine enhanced training capability with the light strike task.

Dimensions: Span, 27 ft 8 in (8,43 m); Length, 30 ft 6$\frac{1}{2}$ in (9,31 m); height, 12 ft 5$\frac{1}{2}$ in (3,80 m); wing area, 135·63 sq ft (12,60 m²).

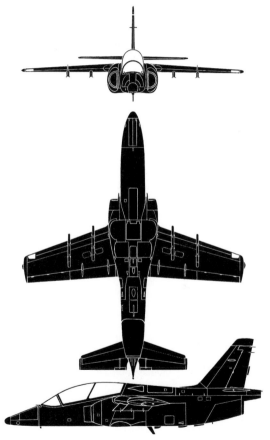

SIAI MARCHETTI SF 600TP CANGURO

Country of Origin: Italy.

Type: Light utility transport.

Power Plant: Two 420 shp Allison 250-B17C turboprops.

Performance: Max cruise speed, 190 mph (306 km/h) at 5,000 ft (1 525 m); cruise (75% power), 178 mph (287 km/h) at 10,000 ft (3 050 m); max initial climb, 1,515 ft/min (7,7 m/sec); service ceiling, 24,000 ft (7 315 m); range (max payload), 372 mls (600 km), (max internal fuel), 981 mls (1 580 km), (plus two 66 Imp gal/300 l external tanks), 1,398 mls (2 250 km).

Weights: Operational empty, 4,292 lb (1 947 kg); max take-off, 8,157 lb (3 700 kg).

Accommodation: Pilot and co-pilot/passenger on flight deck and provision for up to nine passengers in main cabin. Optional internal arrangements for six passengers in corporate transport version, four stretcher patients and two medical attendants in aeromedical version, and 12 paratroops in military transport version.

Status: The SF 600TP was first flown on 8 April 1981 (this being the original F 600 with piston engines replaced by turboprops), a third prototype flown in August 1984 featuring a retractable undercarriage. The SF 600 was being offered at the beginning of 1987 with both fixed and retractable undercarriages. An initial production batch of nine aircraft was under construction at the beginning of 1987.

Notes: The SF 600TP Canguro (Kangaroo) is being offered for a variety of roles, ranging from coastal surveillance with 360 deg ventral radar, photogrammetry (with optional high-precision navigation system) and agricultural spraying and dusting with external tank or hopper. A dedicated freighter version is also on offer.

SIAI MARCHETTI SF 600TP CANGURO

Dimensions: Span, 49 ft 2½ in (15,00 m); length, 39 ft 10½ in (12,15 m); height, 15 ft 1 in (4,60 m); wing area, 258·3 sq ft (24,00 m²).

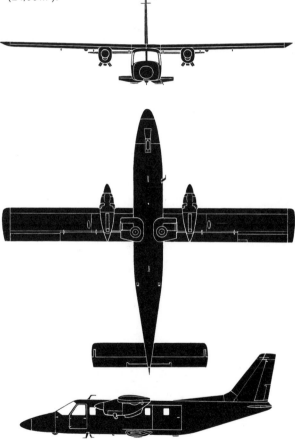

SUKHOI SU-24 (FENCER)

Country of Origin: USSR.

Type: Deep penetration interdictor and strike aircraft.

Power Plant: Two (estimated) 16,975 lb st (7 000 kgp) dry and 24,250 lb st (11 000 kgp) Lyulka or Tumansky turbojets.

Performance: (Estimated) Max speed (without external stores), 1,440 mph (2 317 km/h) above 36,000 ft (11 000 m), or Mach = 2·18, 915 mph (1 470 km/h) at sea level, or Mach = 1·2; combat radius (with 4,400 lb/2 000 kg of ordnance and two jettisonable tanks), 1,115 mls (1 795 km) HI-LO-HI, 345 mls (555 km) LO-LO-LO; service ceiling, 54,135 ft (16 500 m).

Weights: (Estimated) Empty equipped, 41,890 lb (19 000 kg); max take-off, 87,000 lb (39 500 kg).

Armament: one 30-mm cannon and up to 17,635 lb (8 000 kg) of ordnance on four fuselage hardpoints (two in tandem and two side by side) and four wing hardpoints (two swivelling on the outer panels and two on fixed glove).

Status: Prototype believed flown 1970, with initial operational status achieved late 1974. Now assigned primarily to the strategic role with some 450 equipping regiments (strategic bombing and deep strike) in five air armies.

Notes: The latest variant of the Su-24 is the Fencer-D (illustrated), which, first introduced in 1983, differs externally from the preceding Fencer-C in having a lengthened nose, a conventional probe and large aerodynamic fences above the inboard weapon pylons. The Fencer-C (see 1986 edition) embodied equipment changes and different engines to those powering the -A and -B. The Su-24 was the first Soviet aircraft in its category to carry a weapons systems officer, and has a large pulse-Doppler radar with a 50-in (1,27-m) diam scanner dish.

SUKHOI SU-24 (FENCER)

Dimensions: (Estimated) Span (16 deg sweep), 56 ft 6 in (17,25 m), (68 deg sweep), 33 ft 9 in (10,30 m); length (excluding probes), 65 ft 6 in (20,00 m); height, 18 ft 0 in (5,50 m); wing area, 452 sq ft (42,00 m²).

SUKHOI SU-25 (FROGFOOT)

Country of Origin: USSR.

Type: Single-seat attack and close air support aircraft.

Power Plant: Two 11,240 lb st (5 100 kgp) Tumansky R-13-300 turbojets.

Performance: (Estimated) Max speed (without external stores), 545 mph (877 km/h) at 10,000 ft (3 050 m) or Mach = 0·757; combat radius (with 8,820 lb/4 000 kg of ordnance and allowance for 30 min loiter at 5,000 ft/1 525 m), 340 mls (547 km) HI-LO-LO-HI; ferry range (with four 108 Imp gal/490 l external tanks), 1,800 mls (2 895 km).

Weights: Empty, 20,950 lb (9 500 kg); max take-off, 41,890–44,090 lb (19 000–20 000 kg).

Armament: One 30-mm cannon and up to 8,820 lb (4 000 kg) of ordnance on 10 wing hardpoints, including 57-mm and 80-mm unguided rockets, 1,100-lb (500-kg) retarded cluster bombs, etc. Air-to-air missiles for self defence may be carried on outboard hardpoints.

Status: The Su-25 was first observed under test in the late 'seventies, prototypes having presumably flown during 1977–78, with initial deliveries to the Soviet Air Forces following in 1980–81. The first export customer for the Su-25 was Czechoslovakia, and production was continuing at the beginning of 1987 at Tbilisi at a rate of 100 aircraft annually.

Notes: The Su-25 is broadly comparable with the USAF's Fairchild A-10A Thunderbolt II. It features a levered-suspension type undercarriage with low-pressure tyres suitable for rough field operation and wingtip fairings of flattened ovoid section which incorporate split spoilers operated symmetrically or differentially to aid low-altitude manœuvrability. A two-seat operational training version is designated Su-25UB. Operators of the Su-25 include Hungary and Iraq.

SUKHOI SU-25 (FROGFOOT)

Dimensions: (Estimated) Span, 46 ft 7 in (14,20 m); length (including nose probes), 49 ft $10\frac{1}{2}$ in (15,20 m); height, 15 ft $8\frac{9}{10}$ in (4,80 m). Wing area, 404·74 sq ft (37,60 m²).

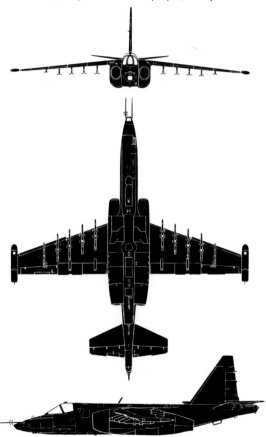

SUKHOI SU-27 (FLANKER)

Country of Origin: USSR.
Type: Single-seat multi-role fighter.
Power Plant: Two (estimated) 20,000 lb st (9 070 kgp) dry and 30,000 lb st (13 610 kgp) reheat turbofans.
Performance: (Estimated) Max speed, 1,520 mph (1 445 km/h) above 36,100 ft (11 000 m), or Mach = 2·3, 835 mph (1 345 km/h) at sea level, or Mach = 1·1; initial climb, 60,000 ft/min (304,5 m/sec); tactical radius (subsonic area intercept with external fuel and four AAMs) 930 mls (1 500 km).
Weights: (Estimated) Empty equipped, 39,000 lb (17 690 kg); loaded (air-air mission), 44,000 lb (19 960 kg); max take-off, 63 500 lb (28 805 kg).
Armament: Up to six AA-10 medium-range semi-active radar-guided medium-range AAMs, or up to 13,200 lb (5 990 kg) of air-ground weaponry for attack mission.
Status: The Su-27 was first seen at Ramenskoye in 1977, and is believed to have entered production at Komsomolsk in 1981, reportedly achieving initial operational capability early in 1986, with approximately 100 in service by the beginning of 1987.
Notes: The Su-27 is generally comparable with the F-15 Eagle and possesses a fundamentally similar configuration to that of the smaller and lighter MiG-29 Fulcrum. It is primarily an all-weather counterair fighter with secondary attack capability, and possesses track-while-scan radar, a pulse-Doppler lookdown/shootdown weapon system, infrared search and tracking, and a digital data link.

SUKHOI SU-27 (FLANKER)

Dimensions: (Estimated) Span, 46 ft 0 in (14,00 m); length, 60 ft 0 in (21,00 m); wing area, 538 sq ft (50,00 m²).

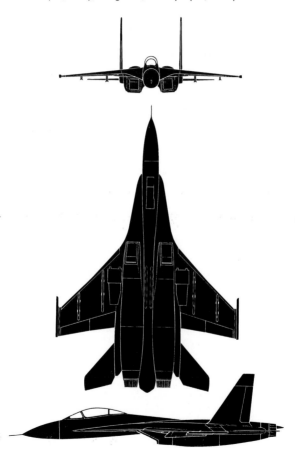

TUPOLEV TU-22M (BACKFIRE-B)

Country of Origin: USSR.

Type: Medium-range strategic bomber and maritime strike/reconnaissance aircraft.

Power Plant: Two (estimated) 33,070 lb st (15 000 kgp) dry and 46,300 lb st (21 000 kgp) reheat Kuznetsov turbofans.

Performance: (Estimated) Max speed (short-period dash), 1,265 mph (2 036 km/h) or Mach = 1·91 at 39,370 ft (12 000 m), (sustained), 1,056 mph (1 700 km/h) or Mach = 1·6 at 39,370 ft (12 000 m), 685 mph (1 100 km/h) or Mach = 0·9 at sea level; combat radius (unrefuelled with single AS-4 ASM and high-altitude subsonic mission profile), 2,610 mls (4 200 km); max unrefuelled combat range (with 12,345 lb/5 600 kg internal ordnance), 3,420 mls (5 500 km).

Weights: (Estimated) Max take-off, 260,000 lb (118 000 kg).

Armament: Remotely-controlled tail barbette housing twin 23-mm NR-23 cannon. Internal load of free-falling weapons up to 12,345 lb (5 600 kg) or one AS-4 Kitchen inertially-guided stand-off missile housed semi-externally.

Status: Flight testing of initial prototype commenced late 1969, with pre-production series of up to 12 aircraft following in 1972–73. Initial version (Backfire-A) was built in small numbers only. Initial operational capability attained with Backfire-B in 1975–76, production rate of 30 annually being attained in 1977 and remaining constant at beginning of 1987, when 190–200 were in service with Soviet Long-range Aviation and a similar quantity with the Soviet Naval Air Force. An advanced version, the Backfire-C, with redesigned engine air intakes and presumably uprated engines has been reported under test, but its production status is uncertain.

TUPOLEV TU-22M (BACKFIRE-B)

Dimensions: (Estimated) Span (20 deg sweep), 115 ft 0 in (35,00 m), (55 deg sweep), 92 ft 0 in (28,00 m); length, 138 ft 0 in (42,00 m); height, 29 ft 6 in (9,00 m); wing area, 1,830 sq ft (170,00 m²).

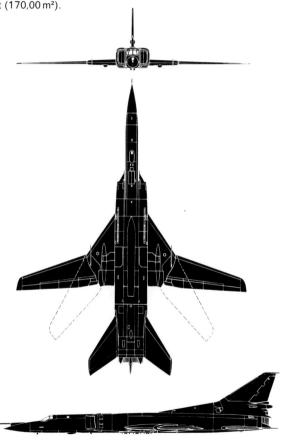

TUPOLEV TU-142M (BEAR-H)

Country of Origin: USSR.

Type: Long-range strategic bomber and cruise missile carrier.

Power Plant: Four 14,795 ehp Kuznetsov NK-12MV turbo-props.

Performance: Max (over target) speed, 528 mph (850 km/h) at 40,000 ft (12 190 m), or Mach = 0·8; max continuous cruise, 440 mph (708 km/h) at 36,090 ft (11 000 m), or Mach = 0·67; max unrefuelled range, 7,800 mls (12 550 km) with 25,000-lb (11 340-kg) warload; max unrefuelled combat radius, 5,157 mls (8 300 km) with 11,025-lb (5 000-kg) warload.

Weights: (Estimated) Max take-off, 418,870 lb (190 000 kg).

Armament: Twin 23-mm cannon in tail barbette. Up to eight AS-15 1,865-mile (3 000-km) range cruise missile (two paired on each of two pylons between fuselage and inboard engine nacelles and four in weapons bays) or up to 22,045 lb (10 000 kg) of free-falling weapons.

Status: The Bear-H entered production at Taganrog in 1982, and, based on the Tu-142 Bear-F airframe, achieved initial operational capability in 1984, with approximately 40–45 in service by beginning of 1987.

Notes: The airframe of the Bear-H is fundamentally similar to that of the late-production Bear-F maritime aircraft with the revised flight deck (18 in/46 cm longer) feature of this model, but lacking the (5 ft/1,52 m) lengthening of the forward fuselage. The Bear-F (of which some 55 in service with the Soviet Navy) is the optimised maritime derivative of the Tu-95 Bear first flown in September 1954. Principal among numerous changes introduced included a structurally and aerodynamically redesigned wing. The original production Bear-B and -C models have been reconfigured for the AS-4 Kitchen missile as Bear-Gs.

TUPOLEV TU-142M (BEAR-H)

Dimensions: Span, 167 ft 6 in (51,05 m); length, 164 ft 6 in (50,14 m); height, 40 ft 0 in (12,15 m); wing area, 3,342·3 sq ft (310,50 m²).

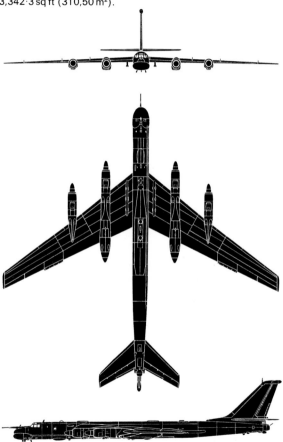

TUPOLEV (BLACKJACK-A)

Country of Origin: USSR.

Type: Long-range strategic bomber and maritime strike/reconnaissance aircraft.

Power Plant: Four (approx) 30,000 lb st (13 610 kgp) dry and 50,000 lb st (22 680 kgp) reheat turbofans.

Performance: (Estimated) Max (over-target dash) speed, 1,380 mph (2 220 km/h) at 40,000 ft (12 200 m), or Mach = 2·09; range cruise, 595 mph (960 km/h) at 45,000 ft (13 720 m), or Mach = 0·9; unrefuelled combat radius, 4,540 mls (7 300 km).

Weights: (Estimated) Empty, 260,000 lb (117 950 kg); max take-off, 590,000 lb (267 625 kg).

Armament: Primary weapons are expected to be 1,850-mile (3 000-km) range AS-15 subsonic low-altitude cruise missile and the supersonic BL-10 missile, but provision will be made for free-falling bombs or mix of missiles and bombs up to an estimated maximum of 36,000 lb (16 330 kg).

Status: First seen under test (at Ramenskoye, near Moscow) in 1979, the Blackjack apparently entered production at Kazan in 1984–85, and initial operational capability is anticipated in 1988.

Notes: Blackjack is expected to initially replace the Bear-A in the Soviet strategic bombing force, supplementing Bear-H. Some 25 per cent larger than the Rockwell B-1B, Blackjack was initially known by the provisional reporting designation of Ram-P (indicating that it had first been seen at Ramenskoye). It is anticipated that a series of about 100 bombers of this type will be built at a massive new complex that has been constructed at Kazan.

TUPOLEV (BLACKJACK-A)

Dimensions: (Estimated) Span (minimum sweep), 150 ft 0 in (54,00 m), (maximum sweep), 101 ft 0 in (30,75 m); length, 175 ft 0 in (53,35 m); wing area, 2,500 sq ft (232,25 m²).

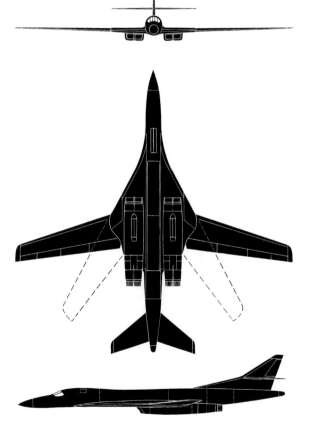

TUPOLEV TU-154M (CARELESS)

Country of Origin: USSR.
Type: Medium-haul commercial transport.
Power Plant: Three 23,380 lb st (10 605 kgp) Soloviev D-30KU-154 II turbofans.
Performance: Max cruising speed, 590 mph (950 km/h) at 39,040 ft (11 900 m); econ cruise, 528 mph (850 km/h) at 29,500–42,650 ft (9 000–13 000 m); range (with 39,680-lb/18 000-kg payload), 2,324 mls (3 740 km), (with 26,455-lb/12 000-kg payload), 3,230 mls (5 200 km), (with 12,015-lb/5 450-kg payload), 4,100 mls (6 600 km).
Weights: Empty, 121,913 lb (55 300 kg); max take-off, 220,460 lb (100 000 kg).
Accommodation: Flight crew of three and basic arrangement for 164 passengers three abreast with single aisle and optional arrangements for 180 economy-class passengers or 162 passengers in mix of first, tourist and economy-class seating.
Status: The Tu-154M entered flight test mid-1982, with initial customer deliveries (to Aeroflot) following from December 1984. In addition to Aeroflot, the Tu-154M has been ordered by CAAC, CSA, Balkan, Cubana, LOT and Syrianair. Production continuing at the beginning of 1987.
Notes: The Tu-154M is fundamentally a re-engined and modernised (revised navigation system with triplex INS, revised slats and spoilers, redesigned tailplane, etc) derivative of the Tu-154B-2 which was the final production model with Kuznetsov NK-8-2 turbofans. The first of six prototype and pre-series Tu-154s was flown on 4 October 1968, the original Tu-154 being superseded by the Tu-154A (1973) and Tu-154B (1977). More than 350 Tu-154s (all versions) delivered.

TUPOLEV TU-154M (CARELESS)

Dimensions: Span, 123 ft 2½ in (37,55 m); length, 157 ft 5¾ in (48,00 m); height, 37 ft 4¾ in (11,40 m); wing area, 2,169 sq ft (201·45 m²).

VALMET L-90 TP REDIGO

Country of Origin: Finland.

Type: Side-by-side two-seat primary/basic trainer.

Power Plant: One 360 shp Allison 250-B17D turboprop.

Performance: (At 2,976 lb/1 350 kg) Max speed, 208 mph (335 km/h) at 9,840 ft (3 000 m); max initial climb, 2,008 ft/min (10,2 m/sec); time to 9,840 ft (3 000 m), 5·5 min; range (max fuel and 30 min reserve), 870 (plus) mls (1 400 plus km).

Weights: Empty equipped, 1,962 lb (890 kg); max take-off, 4,189 lb (1 900 kg).

Armament: (Weapons training and light strike) Max external load of 1,764 lb (800 kg) distributed between six wing stations, typical loads as a single-seater including four 330·5-lb (150-kg) bombs or two 551-lb (250-kg) bombs, plus two flare pods.

Status: The first prototype Redigo was flown in June 1986, with a second prototype scheduled to fly in the autumn of 1987.

Notes: The L-90 TP Redigo is fundamentally similar to the L-80 TP (see 1986 edition) flown on 12 February 1985, embodying minor changes to the wing and tail surfaces. Fully aerobatic and stressed for +7*g* and −3·5*g*, the Redigo is one of the lightest of the current generation of turboprop-powered training aircraft, being in a broadly similar category to the ENAER Aucan (see pages 94–95) and being proposed for use in both two- and three-trainer syllabuses. The Redigo is of conventional metal construction, but a composite wing has been under test since December 1985, and is likely to be offered as an option.

VALMET L-90 TP REDIGO

Dimensions: Span, 33 ft 11 in (10,34 m); length, 25 ft 11 in (7,90 m); height, 9 ft 4¼ in (2,85 m); wing area, 158·77 sq ft (14,75 m²).

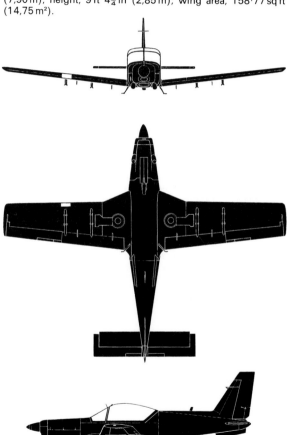

XIAN F-7M (AIRGUARD)

Country of Origin: China (USSR).

Type: Single-seat air superiority and tactical fighter.

Power Plant: One 9,700 lb st (4400 kgp) dry and 13,448 lb st (6100 kgp) Chengdu Wopen-7BM turbojet.

Performance: Max speed, 1,350 mph (2175 km/h) above 36,090 ft (11000 m) or Mach = 2·05; max initial climb, 35,435 ft/min (180 m/sec); service ceiling, 59,710 ft (18200 m); range (internal fuel and two PL-2 AAMs), 745 mls (1200 km), (two PL-7 AAMs and three 110 Imp gal/500 l drop tanks), 1,080 mls (1740 km).

Weights: Empty, 11,629 lb (5275 kg); normal max take-off, 16,603 lb (7531 kg).

Armament: Two 30-mm Type 30-1 cannon and two PL-2 or PL-7 air-to-air missiles on inboard wing stations, or up to four 18 × 57-mm rocket pods, or two 1,100-lb (500-kg) or two 550-lb (250-kg) and two 330-lb (150-kg) bombs.

Status: The F-7 is a reverse-engineered version of the late 'fifties MiG-21F clear-weather air superiority fighter manufactured by the Xian Aircraft Company. Prototype flown (as J-7) December 1964, progressive developments being J-7B (aft-hinging hood, twin cannon and additional weapons pylons) and J-7M (western avionics). Exported to Albania, (F-7B) Egypt, Somalia, Sudan, Zimbabwe, Tanzania, (F-7M) Iraq and Pakistan.

Notes: A two-seat version, the JJ-7 (export designation FT-7), is a combat-capable trainer available with similar equipment to J-7B (export F-7B) or J-7M (F-7M), latter promoted (as Airguard) by Hong Kong-based Aircraft Technology concern. Proposals existed at beginning of 1987 for re-engining as F-7X with western engine.

XIAN F-7M (AIRGUARD)

Dimensions: Span, 23 ft 5⅜ in (7,15 m); length (excluding probe), 45 ft 9 in (13,94 m); height, 13 ft 5½ in (4,10 m); wing area, 247·6 sq ft (23,00 m²).

XIAN Y-7-100

Country of Origin: China (USSR).

Type: Regional commercial transport.

Power Plant: Two 2,790 shp Shanghai Wojiang-5A-1 turboprops.

Performance: Max speed, 322 mph (518 km/h); max cruise, 301 mph (484 km/h) at 13,125 ft (4 000 m); econ cruise, 263 mph (423 km/h) at 19,685 ft (6 000 m); max initial climb, 1,504 ft/min (7,64 m/sec); service ceiling, 28,700 ft (8 750 m); range (52 passengers), 565 mls (910 km), (max standard fuel), 1,180 mls (1 900 km).

Weights: Operational empty, 32,849 lb (14 900 kg); max take-off, 48,060 lb (21 800 kg).

Accommodation: Flight crew of three and standard arrangement for 52 passengers four abreast with central aisle.

Status: The Y-7-100 is an upgraded version of the Y-7, which, in turn, was a reverse-engineered derivative of the 'sixties vintage Antonov An-24 and was initially flown in 1970. Three flight test Y-7s were built, certification not being obtained until 1980, with production deliveries (to CAAC) commencing 1983. Twenty-four Y-7s preceded the Y-7-100 of which four completed by beginning of 1987 against initial order (from CAAC) for 40.

Notes: The Y-7-100 has been reworked (from the Y-7) by the Hong Kong Aircraft Engineering Co (HAECO) with re-engineered cockpit, western avionics, reconfigured interior and winglets to reduce induced drag. The Y-7-200, available from 1988, will offer improved fuel consumption, the Y-7-300 will embody some structural weight reduction and possibly a new wing, and "stretched" and dedicated freighter versions are under study, the latter embodying a rear loading ramp.

XIAN Y-7-100

Dimensions: Span, 97 ft 2¾ in (29,64 m); length, 77 ft 9½ in (23,71 m); height, 28 ft 0¾ in (8,55 m); wing area, 807·3 sq ft (75,00 m²).

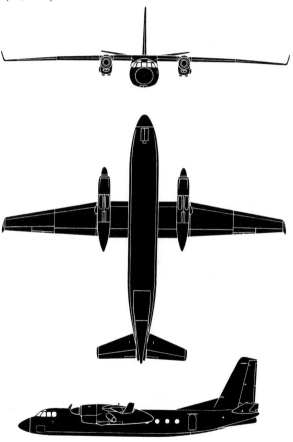

YAKOVLEV YAK-38 (FORGER-A)

Country of Origin: USSR.

Type: Single-seat shipboard air defence and strike fighter.

Power Plant: One 17,985 lb st (8 160 kgp) Lyulka AL-21 lift/cruise turbojet and two tandem-mounted 7,875 lb st (3 570 kgp) Koliesov lift turbojets.

Performance: (Estimated) Max speed, 648 mph (1 042 km/h) or Mach = 0·85 at sea level, 627 mph (1 010 km/h) or Mach = 0·95 above 36,000 ft (10 970 m); max initial climb, 14,750 ft/min (74,93 m/sec); service ceiling, 39,375 ft (12 000 m); combat radius with max ordnance, 150 mls (240 km) LO-LO-LO, 230 mls (370 km) HI-LO-HI, (air defence with two GSh-23 gun pods and two drop tanks), 115 mls (185 km) with 1 hr 15 min on station.

Weights: (Estimated) Empty equipped 16,500 lb (7 485 kg); max take-off, 25,794 lb (11 700 kg).

Armament: (Air Defence) Two AA-8 Aphid AAMs or two podded 23-mm twin-barrel GSh-23 cannon, or (strike) up to 7,936 lb (3 600 kg) of bombs, air-to-surface missiles such as AS-7 Kerry and drop tanks.

Status: Believed to have flown as a prototype in 1971, and initially referred to as the Yak-36MP, the Yak-38 is deployed aboard the carriers *Kiev*, *Minsk*, *Novorossisk* and *Kharkov*, each vessel having a complement of 12 fighters of this type.

Notes: The Yak-38 is capable of rolling vertical take-offs as distinct from orthodox short take-offs which benefit from wing-induced lift, such RVTOs not usually exceeding 35 mph (56 km/h). Primary operational tasks are fleet air defence against shadowing maritime surveillance aircraft, reconnaissance and anti-ship strike.

YAKOVLEV YAK-38 (FORGER-A)

Dimensions: (Estimated) Span, 24 ft 7 in (7,50 m); length, 52 ft 6 in (16,00 m); height, 11 ft 0 in (3,35 m); wing area, 199·14 sq ft (18,50 m²).

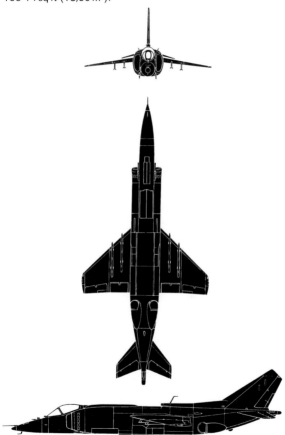

YAKOVLEV YAK-42 (CLOBBER)

Country of Origin: USSR.

Type: Medium-range commercial transport.

Power Plant: Three 14,330 lb st (6 500 kgp) Lotarev D-36 turbofans.

Performance: Max cruising speed, 503 mph (810 km/h at 25,000 ft (7 620 m); econ cruise, 466 mph (750 km/h) at 25,000 ft (7 620 m); range (with max payload), 559 mls (900 km), (with 23,150-lb/10 500-kg payload), 1,242 mls (2 000 km), (with 14,330-lb/6 500-kg payload), 1,864 mls (3 000 km).

Weights: Empty, 63,845 lb (28 960 kg); max take-off, 117,950 lb (53 500 kg).

Accommodation: Crew of two on flight deck and single-class cabin with 120 seats six abreast with central aisle.

Status: First of three prototypes flown on 7 March 1975, and production of initial series of 200 initiated at Smolensk in 1978, with 10 flown by mid-1981. Withdrawn from service for unspecified reason in 1982, but restored to Aeroflot routes in 1984, when production was resumed.

Notes: At the beginning of 1987, development was in process of a "stretched" version of the basic design designated Yak-42M. This features a 14 ft 9 in (4,50 m) longer fuselage to accommodate 156–168 passengers, max take-off weight being increased to 145,000 lb (66 000 kg). The engines of the Yak-42M are 16,550 lb st (7 500 kgp) Lotarev D-436 turbofans and payload over a 1,550-mile (2 500-km) range is claimed to be 35,275 lb (16 000 kg). The Yak-42 programme has suffered a number of delays resulting from unspecified causes, but production for Aeroflot is now continuing at Smolensk of both the basic Yak-42 and the stretched Yak-42M, the latter being scheduled to enter service during the course of this year.

YAKOVLEV YAK-42 (CLOBBER)

Dimensions: Span, 114 ft 5¼ in (34,88 m); length, 119 ft 4¼ in (36,38 m); height, 32 ft 1¾ in (9,80 m); wing area, 1,615 sq ft (150,00 m²).

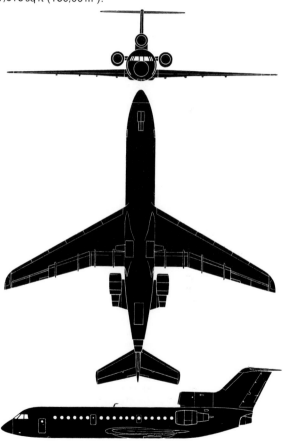

AEROSPATIALE AS 332M1 SUPER PUMA

Country of Origin: France.
Type: Medium tactical transport helicopter.
Power Plant: Two 1,877 shp Turboméca Makila 1A1 turbo-shafts.
Performance: (At 19,840 lb/9 00 kg) Max speed, 173 mph (278 km/h); max cruise, 163 mph (262 km/h) at sea level; max inclined climb, 1,397 ft/min (7,1 m/sec); hovering ceiling (in ground effect), 8,856 ft (2 700 m), (out of ground effect), 5,248 ft (1 600 m); range, 523 mls (842 km).
Weights: Empty, 9,745 lb (4 420 kg); max take-off, 19,840 lb (9 000 kg), (with external load), 20,615 lb (9 350 kg).
Dimensions: Rotor diam, 51 ft 9¾ in (15,60 m); fuselage length, 48 ft 7¾ in (14,82 m).
Notes: The stretched version of the AS 332 was first flown on 10 October 1980, uprated versions of the military (AS 332M1) and civil (AS 332L1) versions being introduced in 1986. More than 200 Super Pumas had been delivered by the end of 1986 when orders totalled in excess of 260. The AS 332F is a navalised ASW version with an overall length of 42 ft 1⅓ in (12,83 m) with rotor blades folded. Licence manufacture of the Super Puma is being undertaken in Indonesia as the NAS-332, and production by the parent company was continuing at a rate of four monthly at the beginning of 1987. The AS 332L can accommodate up to 22 passengers and the AS 332M can carry 25 troops and can be armed with 20-mm cannon or rocket launchers.

AEROSPATIALE AS 350L1 ECUREUIL

Country of Origin: France.
Type: Military six-seat general-purpose helicopter.
Power Plant: One 693 shp Turboméca Arriel 1D turboshaft.
Performance: (At 4,850 lb/2 200 kg) Max speed, 169 mph (272 km/h); max cruise, 149 mph (240 km/h); normal cruise, 137 mph (220 km/h); max inclined climb, 1,500 ft/min (7,5 m/sec); hovering ceiling (in ground effect), 9,400 ft (2 870 m), (out of ground effect), 6,300 ft (1 920 m); range, 407 mls (655 km).
Weights: Empty, 2,575 lb (1 168 kg); max take-off, 4,850 lb (2 200 kg), (with external load), 5,400 lb (2 450 kg).
Dimensions: Rotor diam, 35 ft 0¾ in (10,69 m); fuselage length (tail rotor included), 35 ft 10⅓ in (10,93 m).
Notes: The AS 350L1 is the current military version of the single-engined Ecureuil (Squirrel). The Ecureuil was first flown on 27 June 1974 with a 615 shp Avco Lycoming LTS 101-600A2 turboshaft with which it is marketed in the USA as the AStar, the first Arriel-powered helicopter flying on 14 February 1975. The first AS 350L1 was flown in March 1985 with initial deliveries commencing in March 1986, and offers improved hot-and-high performance and an increased useful load. More than 950 single-engined Ecureuils (and AStars) had been delivered by the beginning of 1987, when production of both single- and twin-engined models (see page 216) was continuing at a rate of eight monthly. The AStar version is assembled and finished by Aérospatiale in Alberta.

AEROSPATIALE AS 355F2 ECUREUIL 2

Country of Origin: France.
Type: Six-seat light general-purpose utility helicopter.
Power Plant: Two 420 shp Allison 250-C20F turboshafts.
Performance: (At 5,600 lb/2 540 kg) Max speed, 169 mph (272 km/h); normal cruise, 139 mph (224 km/h); max inclined climb, 1,300 ft/min (6,5 m/sec); hovering ceiling (in ground effect), 5,900 ft (1 800 m), (out of ground effect), 4,430 ft (1 350 m); range, 438 mls (705 km).
Weights: Empty, 2,877 lb (1 305 kg); max take-off, 5,600 lb (2 540 kg), (with external load), 5,732 lb (2 600 kg).
Dimensions: Rotor diam, 35 ft 0¾ in (10,69 m); fuselage length (tail rotor included), 35 ft 10⅓ in (10,93 m).
Notes: Flown for the first time on 27 September 1979, the Ecureuil 2 employs an essentially similar airframe and similar dynamic components to those of the single-engined AS 350 Ecureuil (see page 215). From 1986, the production models have been the AS 355F2 (civil) and AS 355M2 (military) offering increased maximum take-off weights by comparison with preceding production models. The AS 355M2 can be armed with a 20-mm cannon and rocket launchers for the fire support role. By the beginning of 1987, more than 400 Ecureuil 2 and TwinStar (the latter being the name applied for the North American market) helicopters had been ordered. The AS 355M has been ordered by the *Armée de l'Air* and the French Army, and may be fitted with a TOW installation. Some 200 TwinStars sold in North America.

AÉROSPATIALE SA 365 DAUPHIN 2

Country of Origin: France.
Type: Multi-purpose and transport helicopter.
Power Plant: Two 700 shp Turboméca Arriel 1 C turboshafts.
Performance: (SA 365N) Max speed, 190 mph (305 km/h); max continuous cruise, 173 mph (278 km/h) at sea level; max inclined climb, 1,279 ft/min (6,5 m/sec); hovering ceiling (in ground effect), 3,296 ft (1 005 m), (out of ground effect), 3,116 ft (950 m); range, 548 mls (882 km) at sea level.
Weights: Empty, 4,511 lb (2 47 kg); max take-off, 8,818 lb (4 000 kg).
Dimensions: Rotor diam, 39 ft 1½ in (11,93 m); fuselage length (including tail rotor), 37 ft 6⅓ in (11,44 m).
Notes: Flown as a prototype on 31 March 1979, the SA 365 is the latest derivative of the basic Dauphin (see 1982 edition), and is being manufactured in four versions, the 10–14-seat commercial SA 365N, the military SA 365M Panther (see page 218), the navalised SA 365F with folding rotor, Agrion radar and four AS 15TT anti-ship missiles (20 ordered by Saudi Arabia for delivery from 1984) and the SA 366G, an Avco Lycoming LTS 101-750-powered search and rescue version for the US Coast Guard as the HH-65A Seaguard. Ninety of the last version have been procured by the US Coast Guard, with completion in 1985. Production of the SA 365N was five monthly at the beginning of 1987 when about 280 had been delivered against total orders for some 370 Dauphin helicopters (all versions).

AEROSPATIALE SA 365M PANTHER

Country of Origin: France.
Type: Multirole tactical helicopter.
Power Plant: Two 912 shp Turboméca TM 333-1M turbo-shafts.
Performance: (At 9,039 lb/4 100 kg) Max speed, 184 mph (296 km/h); max cruise, 170 mph (274 km/h) at sea level; max inclined climb, 1,575 ft/min (8 m/sec); hovering ceiling (in ground effect), 10,500 ft (3 200 m), (out of ground effect), 8,200 ft (2 500 m); range, 485 mls (780 km).
Weights: Empty, 5,070 lb (2 300 kg); max take-off, 9,039 lb (4 100 kg).
Dimensions: Rotor diam, 39 ft 1½ in (11,93 m); fuselage length (including tail rotor), 39 ft 7 in (12,07 m).
Notes: A military derivative of the Dauphin 2 (see page 217), the first prototype of the SA 365M Panther was flown in February 1984, with the first of two additional prototypes being scheduled to fly during the spring of 1987. The Panther is intended for armed and light tactical transport missions. In the armed role it will use a Viviane roof-mounted day/night sight and weapon options include 20-mm Giat cannon in pods, pods of 22 68-mm rockets, eight Matra Mistral air-air missiles for anti-helicopter operations, or eight Hot anti-armour missiles. As an assault transport the Panther will accommodate 8–10 commandos, and provision is made for armour-plated seats, the armour protection of vital parts and jet diluters. The basic model has crash-worthy tanks and an instrument panel with CRT display.

AGUSTA A 109A MK II

Country of Origin: Italy.

Type: Eight-seat light utility helicopter.

Power Plant: Two 420 shp Allison 250-C20B turboshafts.

Performance: (At 5,402 lb/2 450 kg) Max speed, 193 mph (311 km/h); max continuous cruise, 173 mph (278 km/h); range cruise, 143 mph (231 km/h); max inclined climb rate, 1,820 ft/min (9,25 m/sec); hovering ceiling (in ground effect), 9,800 ft (2 987 m), (out of ground effect), 6,800 ft (2 073 m); max range, 356 mls (573 km).

Weights: Empty equipped, 3,125 lb (1 418 kg); max take-off, 5,730 lb (2 600 kg).

Dimensions: Rotor diam, 36 ft 1 in (11,00 m); fuselage length, 35 ft 2½ in (10,73 m).

Notes: The A 109A Mk II is an improved model of the basic A 109A, the first of four prototypes of which flew on 4 August 1971, with customer deliveries commencing late 1976. Some 280 A 109As had been ordered by the beginning of 1987. The Mk II, which supplanted the initial model in production during 1981, has been the subject of numerous detail improvements, the transmission rating of the combined engines being increased from 692 to 740 shp, and the maximum continuous rating of each engine from 385 to 420 shp. An anti-armour version has been procured by Argentine, Libyan and Yugoslav forces. In 1984, a "widebody" version of the A 109 Mk II was introduced. Flown in September of that year, this has new side panels adding 8 in (20 cm) to the cabin width. A coastal patrol version is illustrated above.

AGUSTA A 129 MANGUSTA

Country of Origin: Italy.

Type: Two-seat light attack helicopter.

Power Plant: Two 915 shp Rolls-Royce Gem 2 Mk 1004D turboshafts.

Performance: (Estimated) Max speed, 173 mph (278 km/h); cruise (TOW configuration at 8,377 lb/3 800 kg), 149 mph (240 km/h) at 5,740 ft (1 750 m); max inclined climb (at 8,377 lb/3 800 kg), 2,087 ft/min (10,6 m/sec); hovering ceiling at 8,090 lb/3 670 kg), (in ground effect), 10,795 ft (3 290 m), (out of ground effect), 7,840 ft (2 390 m).

Weights: Mission, 8,080 lb (3 665 kg); max take-off, 8,377 lb (3 800 kg).

Dimensions: Rotor diam, 39 ft 0½ in (11,90 m); fuselage length, 40 ft 3¼ in (12,27 m).

Notes: The A 129 Mangusta (Mongoose) dedicated attack and anti-armour helicopter with full night/bad weather combat capability has been developed to an Italian Army requirement. The first of five flying prototypes commenced flight test on 15 September 1983, and first deliveries are scheduled for 1987, with 60 expected to be funded for the Italian Army and 20 ordered during 1986 for the Netherlands Army. In typical anti-armour configuration, the A 129 will be armed with eight TOW missiles to which can be added 2·75-in (7-cm) rocket launchers for suppressive fire. The fourth prototype, flown in March 1985, has a unified electronic control system, combining flight controls, and weapon aiming and firing systems.

220

ATLAS ALPHA XH-1

Country of Origin: South Africa.
Type: Tandem two-seat light attack helicopter.
Power Plant: One 870 shp Turboméca Artouste IIIB turbo-shaft.
Performance: (Estimated) Max speed, 125 mph (200 km/h) at sea level; max inclined climb, 900 ft/min (4,5 m/sec); combat radius, 170 mls (275 km).
Weights: Empty, 3,086 lb (1 400 kg); max take-off, 4,850 lb (2 200 kg).
Dimensions: Rotor diam, 36 ft 1¾ in (11,02 m); length (overall), 42 ft 1½ in (12,84 m).
Notes: The Alpha XH-1 has been developed by the Atlas Aircraft Corporation on the basis on the Aérospatiale SA 316B Alouette III, employing fundamentally similar rotor and transmission systems. Produced to a South African Air Force contract awarded in March 1981, the Alpha XH-1 was flown for the first time on 3 February 1985. Further development is expected to include the introduction of stub-wings or outriggers for the carriage of anti-armour weapons which will augment the 20-mm single-barrel GA1 cannon, the flexible mounting of which permits 120 deg traverse port and starboard, 10 deg elevation and 60 deg depression. The current fashion in crew disposition for attack helicopters is followed, with the pilot occupying the rear cockpit. No details relating to production plans have been revealed, but the South African Air Force has a requirement for a substantial number of helicopters in its category.

BELL AH-1S HUEYCOBRA

Country of Origin: USA.

Type: Two-seat light attack helicopter.

Power Plant: One 1,800 shp Avco Lycoming T53-L-703 turboshaft.

Performance: Max speed, 172 mph (277 km/h), (TOW configuration), 141 mph (227 km/h); max inclined climb, 1,620 ft/min (8,23 m/sec); hovering ceiling TOW configuration (in ground effect), 12,200 ft (3 720 m); max range, 357 mls (574 km).

Weights: (TOW configuration) Operational empty, 6,479 lb (2 939 kg); max take-off, 10,000 lb (4 535 kg).

Dimensions: Rotor diam, 44 ft 0 in (13,41 m); fuselage length, 44 ft 7 in (13,59 m).

Notes: The AH-1S is a dedicated attack and anti-armour helicopter serving primarily with the US Army which had received 297 new-production AH-1S HueyCobras by mid-1981, plus 290 resulting from the conversion of earlier AH-1G and AH-1Q HueyCobras. Current planning calls for conversion of a further 372 AH-1Gs to AH-1S standards, and both conversion and new-production AH-1S HueyCobras have been progressively upgraded to "Modernised AH-1S" standard, the entire programme having been completed in 1985, resulting in a total of 959 "Modernised" AH-1S HueyCobras. The AH-1S is being licence-built in Japan by Fuji for the Ground Self-Defence Force which is to receive 54 examples, and the AH-1S has also been supplied to Israel and Pakistan (as illustrated above).

BELL AH-1W SUPERCOBRA

Country of Origin: USA.
Type: Two-seat light attack helicopter.
Power Plant: Two 1,693 shp General Electric T700-GE-401 turboshafts.
Performance: Max cruising speed, 184 mph (296 km/h) at 3,000 ft (915 m); hovering ceiling (out of ground effect), 10,000 ft (3 050 m); range, 380 mls (611 km) at 3,000 ft (915 m).
Weights: Empty, 9,700 lb (4 400 kg); max take-off, 14,750 lb (6 691 kg).
Dimensions: Rotor diam, 48 ft 0 in (14,63 m); fuselage length, 45 ft 3 in (13,79 m).
Notes: Flown for the first time on 16 November 1983, the AH-1W SuperCobra is an enhanced-capability derivative of the AH-1T SeaCobra (see 1984 edition) of the US Marine Corps. The first of an initial batch of 22 SuperCobras was delivered to the USMC in March 1986, and a follow-on batch of a further 22 was ordered September 1985. Current USMC planning calls for modification of 44 AH-1Ts to -1W standard and procurement of 34 more newbuild -1Ws from Fiscal 1987 funding. More powerful and more heavily armed than the SeaCobra, the primary USMC mission of the SuperCobra will be to provide escort for troop-carrying helicopters, and in this role it can augment its 20-mm three-barrel rotary cannon with up to four AIM-9L Sidewinder missiles on the stub-wing pylons. A typical load for the anti-armour mission can comprise eight laser-guided Hellfire launch-and-leave missiles.

BELL MODEL 214ST

Country of Origin: USA.

Type: Medium transport helicopter (20 seats).

Power Plant: Two 1,625 shp (limited to combined output of 2,250 shp) General Electric CT7-2A turboshafts.

Performance: Max cruising speed, 164 mph (264 km/h) at sea level, 161 mph (259 km/h) at 4,000 ft (1 220 m); hovering ceiling (in ground effect), 12,600 ft (3 840 m), (out of ground effect), 3,300 ft (1 005 m); range (standard fuel), 460 mls (740 km).

Weights: Max take-off (internal or external load), 17,500 lb (7 938 kg).

Dimensions: Rotor diam, 52 ft 0 in (15,85 m); fuselage length, 50 ft 0 in (15,24 m).

Notes: The Model 214ST (Super Transport) is a significantly improved derivative of the Model 214B BigLifter (see 1978 edition), production of which was phased out early 1981, initial customer deliveries of the Model 214ST beginning early 1982. The Model 214ST test-bed was first flown in March 1977, and the first of three representative prototypes (one in military configuration and two for commercial certification) commenced its test programme in August 1979. Work on an initial series of 100 helicopters of this type commenced in 1981. A version with wheel landing gear was certificated in March 1983, and alternative layouts are available for either 16 or 17 passengers. Military operators include the Venezuelan and Peruvian air forces, and the Royal Thai Army. Four have been supplied to the Republic of China.

BELL MODEL 222B

Country of Origin: USA.

Type: Eight/ten-seat light utility and transport helicopter.

Power Plant: Two 680 shp Avco Lycoming LTS 101-750C-1 turboshafts.

Performance: Max cruising speed, 150 mph (241 km/h) at sea level, 146 mph (235 km/h) at 8,000 ft (2 400 m); max climb, 1,730 ft/min (8,8 m/sec); hovering ceiling (in ground effect), 10,300 ft (3 135 m), (out of ground effect), 6,400 ft (1 940 m); range (no reserves), 450 mls (724 km) at 8,000 ft (2 400 m).

Weights: Empty equipped, 4,577 lb (2 076 kg); max take-off (standard configuration), 8,250 lb (3 742 kg).

Dimensions: Rotor diam, 42 ft 0 in (12,80 m); fuselage length, 39 ft 9 in (12,12 m).

Notes: The first of five prototypes of the Model 222 was flown on 13 August 1976, an initial production series of 250 helicopters of this type being initiated in 1978, with production deliveries commencing in January 1980, and some 160 delivered by beginning of 1987, when production rate was one monthly. Several versions of the Model 222 are on offer or under development, these including an executive version with a flight crew of two and five or six passengers, and the so-called "offshore" model with accommodation for eight passengers and a flight crew of two. The Model 222B has a larger main rotor and uprated power plant, a utility version, the Model 222UT (illustrated), having been certificated mid 1983, with deliveries commencing shortly afterwards.

BELL MODEL 406CS COMBAT SCOUT

Country of Origin: USA.
Type: Light attack and multirole helicopter.
Power Plant: One 650 shp Allison 250-C30L turboshaft.
Performance: Max speed, 143 mph (230 km/h); max cruise, 138 mph (222 km/h); hovering ceiling (in ground effect), 19,800 ft (6035 m), (out of ground effect), 17,100 ft (5212 m); range, 250 mls (402 km).
Weights: Empty, 2,266 lb (1028 kg); max take-off, 4,500 lb (2041 kg).
Dimensions: Rotor diam, 35 ft 0 in (10,67 m); fuselage length, 35 ft 10 in (10,31 m).
Notes: The Model 406CS Combat Scout, first flown in June 1984, is fundamentally a multi-mission version of the US Army's OH-58D Aeroscout (see 1986 edition), the winning contender of the AHIP (Army Helicopter Improvement Program) under which existing OH-58A Kiowa helicopters are being upgraded. The Model 406CS features a quick-change weapon system, carrying 7,62-mm or 0·5-in gun pods, 7,62-mm mini-guns, 70-mm rocket pods and Stinger air-air missiles for the armed scouting role, and up to eight TOW missiles for the anti-armour role. It can accept most of the available state-of-the-art roof-mounted stabilised sighting systems, and its features include IR signature reduction, radar warning and a crash-resistant ballistically tolerant fuel system. Under the AHIP programme, 32 OH-58Ds are expected to be procured from Fiscal 1987 funding to augment 99 purchased from earlier funding.

BELL MODEL 412

Country of Origin: USA.

Type: Fifteen-seat utility transport helicopter.

Power Plant: One 1,800 shp Pratt & Whitney PT6T-3B-1 turboshaft.

Performance: Max speed, 149 mph (240 km/h) at sea level; cruise, 143 mph (230 km/h) at sea level, 146 mph (235 km/h) at 5,000 ft (1 525 m); hovering ceiling (in ground effect), 10,800 ft (3 290 m), (out of ground effect), 7,100 ft (2 165 m) at 10,500 lb/4 763 kg; max range, 282 mls (454 km), (with auxiliary tanks), 518 mls (834 km).

Weights: Empty equipped, 6,535 lb (2 964 kg); max take-off, 11,900 lb (5 397 kg).

Dimensions: Rotor diam, 46 ft 0 in (14,02 m); fuselage length, 41 ft 8½ in (12,70 m).

Notes: The Model 412, flown for the first time in August 1979, is an updated Model 212 (production of which was continuing at the beginning of 1987) with a new-design four-bladed rotor, a shorter rotor mast assembly, and uprated engine and transmission systems, giving more than twice the life of the Model 212 units. Composite rotor blades are used and the rotor head incorporates elastomeric bearings and dampers to simplify moving parts. An initial series of 200 helicopters was laid down with customer deliveries commencing February 1981. Licence manufacture is undertaken by Agusta in Italy, a multi-purpose military version being designated AB 412 Griffon, and production is also being undertaken by IPTN in Indonesia.

BOEING VERTOL 414 CHINOOK

Country of Origin: USA.
Type: Medium transport helicopter.
Power Plant: Two 3,750 shp Avco Lycoming T55-L-712 turboshafts.
Performance: (At 45,400 lb/20 593 kg) Max speed, 146 mph (235 km/h) at sea level; average cruise, 131 mph (211 km/h); max inclined climb, 1,380 ft/min (7,0 m/sec); service ceiling, 8,400 ft (2 560 m); max ferry range, 1,190 mls (1 915 km).
Weights: Empty, 22,591 lb (10 247 kg); max take-off, 50,000 lb (22 680 kg).
Dimensions: Rotor diam (each), 60 ft 0 in (18,29 m); fuselage length, 51 ft 0 in (15,55 m).
Notes: The Model 414 as supplied to the RAF as the Chinook HC Mk 1 combines some features of the US Army's CH-47D (see 1980 edition) and features of the Canadian CH-147, but with provision for glassfibre/carbonfibre rotor blades. The first of 33 Chinook HC Mk 1s for the RAF was flown on 23 March 1980 and accepted on 2 December 1980, with deliveries continuing through 1981, three more being ordered in 1982 and five in 1983. The RAF version can accommodate 44 troops and has three external cargo hooks. During 1981, Boeing Vertol initiated the conversion to essentially similar CH-47D standards a total of 436 CH-47As, Bs and Cs, and this programme is scheduled for completion in 1993. More than 100 Model 414s have been built by Agusta, and 52 are being co-produced by Kawasaki in Japan.

EH INDUSTRIES EH 101

Countries of Origin: United Kingdom and Italy.

Type: Shipboard ant-submarine warfare helicopter and commercial transport and utility helicopter.

Power Plant: Three 1,730 shp General Electric T700-401 (CT7-6A) turboshafts.

Performance: (Estimated) Max cruising speed, 176 mph (283 km/h) at sea level; tactical radius (with 19 troops), 230 mls (370 km); range (commercial transport version with 30 passengers), 633 mls (1 020 km); ferry range, 1,150 mls (1 850 km); endurance (naval version on station with full mission load), 5 hrs.

Weights: Basic empty, 15,500 lb (7 031 kg); max take-off (naval version), 28,660 lb (13 000 kg), (commercial transport), 31,500 lb (14 290 kg).

Dimensions: Rotor diam, 61 ft 0 in (18,59 m); overall length (rotors turning), 75 ft 1½ in (22,90 m).

Notes: EH Industries comprises Westland Helicopters of the UK and Agusta of Italy, the company having been formed specifically for the development of the multi-role EH 101. The first of nine development EH 101s is scheduled to commence flight March–April 1987, the remaining eight being expected to join the test programme within a period of two years, with the fourth and fifth being naval prototypes and the sixth being an army utility version. First deliveries of the commercial version are planned to commence in 1991, with deliveries of the naval version starting in the following year. Final assembly lines are to be established in both the UK and in Italy.

ICA IAR-317 AIRFOX

Country of Origin: Romania.

Type: Two-seat light attack helicopter.

Power Plant: One 858 shp Turboméca Artouste IIIB turboshaft.

Performance: (At 4,850 lb/2 200 kg) Max speed, 136 mph (220 km/h), (with external stores), 125 mph (201 km/h); max cruise (clean), 118 mph (190 km/h); max inclined climb, 886 ft/min (4,50 m/sec); hovering ceiling (in ground effect), 9,350 ft (2 850 m), (out of ground effect), 4,920 ft (1 500 m); max range, 326 mls (525 km), (with auxiliary fuel), 503 mls (810 km).

Weights: Empty, 2,535 lb (1 150 kg); max take-off, 4,850 lb (2 200 kg).

Dimensions: Rotor diam, 36 ft 1¾ in (11,02 m); fuselage length, 32 ft 1¾ in (9,80 m).

Notes: The IAR-317 Airfox has been developed from the licence-built Alouette III (IAR-316B) and the first of three prototypes entered flight test in April 1984. The Airfox is intended primarily for the light ground attack role and its armament includes two fixed 7,62-mm machine guns in the lower front fuselage, a load-carrying beam aft of the rear cockpit having either two or three weapon attachment points on each side. Typical loads (up to a maximum of 1,653 lb/ 750 kg) can include four twin-gun pods, four 110-lb (50-kg) or 220-lb (100-kg) bombs, or four rocket launchers each containing 12 57-mm rockets. Armour protection is provided for the fuel tank and crew seats.

KAMOV KA-27 (HELIX)

Country of Origin: USSR.
Type: (Ka-27) Shipboard anti-submarine warfare and (Ka-32) utility transport helicopter.
Power Plant: Two 2,205 shp Isotov TV3-117V turboshafts.
Performance: (Ka-32) Max speed, 155 mph (250 km/h); max continuous cruise, 143 mph (230 km/h); max range, 497 mls (800 km); service ceiling (at 24,250 lb/11 000 kg), 16,405 ft (5 000 m).
Weights: (Ka-32) Normal loaded, 24,250 lb (11 000 kg); max loaded (with external load), 27,778 lb (12 600 kg).
Dimensions: Rotor diam (each), 52 ft 1⅞ in (15,90 m); overall length, 37 ft 0⅞ in (11,30 m).
Notes: Believed to have flown in prototype form in 1979–80, and first seen in ASW Ka-27 form during Zapad-81 exercises in the Baltic in September 1981, this Kamov helicopter has also been developed for civil roles as the Ka-32, variants including a dedicated search-and-rescue variant, the Ka-32S. The naval Ka-27 and civil Ka-32 appear to differ in no fundamental respect apart from equipment, and the former is now the standard equipment aboard carriers of the Soviet Navy in basic ASW Helix-A form and in Helix-B form for missile target acquisition and mid-course guidance. The Ka-32S is capable of adverse weather and day or night operation, and is equipped with a 661-lb (300-kg) capacity winch for the ASR role. A slung load of up to five *tonnes* (11,023 lb can be lifted by this version). The Helix-C is a SAR and plane guard version of the Ka-27 with a winch on the fuselage portside.

KAMOV (HOKUM)

Country of Origin: USSR.
Type: Tandem two-seat combat helicopter.
Power Plant: Two unidentified turboshafts (possibly related to Isotov TV3-117).
Performance: (Estimated) Max speed, 217 mph (350 km/h); combat radius, 155 mls (250 km).
Weights: (Estimated) Normal loaded, 12,000 lb (5 450 kg).
Dimensions: (Estimated) Rotor diam (each), 59 ft 8 in (18,20 m); length (overall), 52 ft 6 in (16,000 m); height, 17 ft 8 in (5,40 m).
Notes: Possibly the first true air-to-air combat helicopter, intended to eliminate opposing frontline helicopters and presumably featuring a secondary close support role, the Hokum currently possesses no western counterpart. Flight testing of this helicopter is believed to have commenced late 1983 or early 1984, and initial operational capability is anticipated 1987–88. The accompanying illustration should be considered as provisional, but is based on the latest available information and depicts the general configuration. Retaining the superimposed co-axial rotor arrangement which has become the trademark of the Kamov bureau, this dedicated combat helicopter is believed to include a fixed heavy-calibre gun in its armament, underwing pylons being provided for tube-launched missiles for air-air or air-ground use, or anti-armour missiles. Western analysts believe that introduction of Hokum will provide a significant helicopter air superiority capability.

MBB BO 105LS

Country of Origin: Federal Germany.
Type: Five/six-seat light utility helicopter.
Power Plant: Two 550 shp Allison 250-C28C turboshafts.
Performance: Max speed, 168 mph (270 km/h) at sea level; max cruise, 157 mph (252 km/h) at sea level; max climb, 1,970 ft/min (10 m/sec); hovering ceiling (in ground effect), 13,120 ft (4 000 m), (out of ground effect), 11,280 ft (3 440 m); range, 286 mls (460 km).
Weights: Empty, 2,756 lb (1 250 kg); max take-off, 5,291 lb (2 400 kg), (with external load), 5,512 lb (2 500 kg).
Dimensions: Rotor diam, 32 ft 3½ in (9,84 m); fuselage length, 28 ft 1 in (8,56 m).
Notes: The BO 105LS is a derivative of the BO 105CB (see 1979 edition) with uprated transmission and more powerful turboshaft for "hot-and-high" conditions. It is otherwise similar to the BO 105CBS Twin Jet II (420 shp Allison 250-C20B) which was continuing in production at the beginning of 1987, when more than 1,200 BO 105s (all versions) had been delivered and production was running at five monthly, and licence assembly has been undertaken in Indonesia, the Philippines and Spain. Deliveries to the Federal German Army of 227 BO 105M helicopters for liaison and observation tasks commenced late 1979, and deliveries of 212 HOT-equipped BO 105Ps for the anti-armour role began on 4 December 1980 and were completed mid-1984. The latter have uprated engines and transmission systems.

MBB-KAWASAKI BK 117 A-3

Countries of Origin: Federal Germany and Japan.
Type: Multi-purpose eight-to-twelve-seat helicopter.
Power Plant: Two 600 shp Avco Lycoming LTS 101-650B-1 turboshafts.
Performance: Max speed, 171 mph (275 km/h) at sea level; cruise, 164 mph (264 km/h) at sea level; max climb, 1,970 ft/min (10 m/sec); hovering ceiling (in ground effect), 13,450 ft (4 100 m), (out of ground effect), 10,340 ft (3 150 m); range (max payload), 339 mls (545 km).
Weights: Empty, 3,351 lb (1 520 kg); max take-off, 6,173 lb (2 800 kg).
Dimensions: Rotor diam, 36 ft 1 in (11,00 m); fuselage length, 32 ft 5 in (9,88 m).
Notes: The BK 117 is a co-operative development between Messerschmitt-Bölkow-Blohm and Kawasaki, the first of two flying prototypes commencing its flight test programme on 13 June 1979 (in Germany), with the second following on 10 August (in Japan). A decision to proceed with series production was taken in 1980, with first flying on 24 December 1981, and production deliveries commencing first quarter of 1983 in which year 20 were delivered. A further 20 were built in 1984, and production tempo was two monthly at the beginning of 1987. MBB is responsible for the main and tail rotor systems, tail unit and hydraulic components, while Kawasaki is responsible for the fuselage, undercarriage and transmission. The BK 117 A-3M is a purely German multi-role military version for which no orders have been announced.

McDONNELL DOUGLAS 500MD DEFENDER II

Country of Origin: USA.

Type: Light gunship and multi-role helicopter.

Power Plant: One 420 shp Allison 250-C20B turboshaft.

Performance: (At 3,000 lb/1 362 kg) Max speed, 175 mph (282 km/h) at sea level; cruise, 160 mph (257 km/h) at 4,000 ft (1 220 m); max inclined climb, 1,920 ft/min (9,75 m/sec); hovering ceiling (in ground effect), 8,800 ft (2 682 m), (out of ground effect), 7,100 ft (2 164 m); max range, 263 mls (423 km).

Weights: Empty, 1,295 lb (588 kg); max take-off (internal load), 3,000 lb (1 362 kg), (with external load), 3,620 lb (1 642 kg).

Dimensions: Rotor diam, 26 ft 5 in (8,05 m); fuselage length, 21 ft 5 in (6,52 m).

Notes: The Defender II multi-mission version of the Model 500MD was introduced mid-1980 for 1982 delivery, and features a Martin Marietta rotor mast-top sight, a General Dynamics twin-Stinger air-to-air missile pod, an underfuselage 30-mm chain gun and a pilot's night vision sensor. The Defender II can be rapidly reconfigured for anti-armour target designation, anti-helicopter, suppressive fire and transport roles. The Model 500MD TOW Defender (carrying four tube-launched optically-tracked wire-guided anti-armour missiles) is currently in service with Israel (30), South Korea (45) and Kenya (15). Production of the 500 was seven monthly at the beginning of 1987, when upgraded versions, Model 500ME, and MG Paramilitary Defender, were offered.

McDONNELL DOUGLAS 530F

Country of Origin: USA.
Type: Five-seat light utility helicopter.
Power Plant: One 650 shp Allison 250-C30 turboshaft.
Performance: Max cruise speed, 155 mph (250 km/h) at sea level, econ cruise, 150 mph (241 km/h) at 5,000 ft (1 525 m); max inclined climb, 1,780 ft/min (9,04 m/sec); hovering ceiling (in ground effect), 12,000 ft (3 660 m), (out of ground effect), 9,600 ft (2 925 m); range, 269 mls (434 km) at 5,000 ft (1 525 m).
Weights: Max take-off, 3,100 lb (1 406 kg).
Dimensions: Rotor diam, 27 ft 6 in (8,38 m); fuselage length, 23 ft 2½ in (7,07 m).
Notes: The Model 530F is the "hot and high" variant of the Model 500E (see 1983 edition under Hughes 500E) which is characterised by a longer, recontoured nose compared with the preceding Model 500D, offering increased leg room for front seat occupants and a 12 per cent increase in headroom for rear seat passengers. The principal difference between the Models 500E and 530F is the power plant, the former having a 520 shp 250-C20B. The Model 500E was flown on 28 January 1982, and was certificated in November 1982, and the Model 530F was flown in October 1982. Customer deliveries of the Model 530F began in January 1984, and on the following 4 May a military version, the Model 530MG, entered flight test, this being intended primarily for the light attack mission and being essentially similar to the 500ME apart from power plant.

McDONNELL DOUGLAS AH-64 APACHE

Country of Origin: USA.

Type: Tandem two-seat attack helicopter.

Power Plant: Two 1,690 shp General Electric T700-GE-701 turboshafts.

Performance: Max speed, 191 mph (307 km/h); cruise, 179 mph (288 km/h); max inclined climb, 3,200 ft/min (16,27 m/sec); hovering ceiling (in ground effect), 14,600 ft (4 453 m), (out of ground effect), 11,800 ft (3 600 m); service ceiling, 21,000 ft (6 400 m); max range, 424 mls (682 km).

Weights: Empty, 9,900 lb (4 490 kg); primary mission, 13,600 lb (6 169 kg); max take-off, 17,400 lb (7 892 kg).

Dimensions: Rotor diam, 48 ft 0 in (14,63 m); fuselage length, 48 ft 1⅞ in (14,70 m).

Notes: Winning contender in the US Army's AAH (Advanced Attack Helicopter) contest, the AH-64 flew for the first time on 30 September 1975. Two prototypes were used for the initial trials, the first of three more with fully integrated weapons systems commenced trials on 31 October 1979, a further three following in 1980. Planned total procurement comprises 675 AH-64s through 1990, with 593 ordered by beginning of 1987, and a peak production rate of 12 monthly, deliveries having commenced during the summer of 1984 with a total of 180 having been delivered by the beginning of 1987. The AH-64 is armed with a single-barrel 30-mm gun based on the chain-driven bolt system and suspended beneath the forward fuselage, and eight BGM-71A TOW or 16 Hellfire laser-seeking missiles may be carried.

MIL MI-8/17 (HIP)

Country of Origin: USSR.

Type: Assault transport helicopter.

Power Plant: Two (Mi-8) 1,700 shp Isotov TV2-117A or (Mi-17) 1,900 shp TV3-117MT turboshafts.

Performance: Max speed (Mi-8 at 26,455 lb/12 000 kg), 142 mph (230 km/h, (Mi-17 at 28,660 lb/13 000 kg), 155 mph (250 km/h); max cruise (Mi-8), 112 mph (180 km/h), (Mi-17) 149 mph (240 km/h); hovering ceiling (Mi-8 at 24,470 lb/11 100 kg in ground effect), 6,235 ft (1 900 m), (out of ground effect), 2,625 ft (800 m), (Mi-17 at 24,470 lb/11 100 kg out of ground effect), 5,775 ft (1 760 m).

Weights: Empty equipped (typical), 16,007 lb (7 260 kg); max take-off (Mi-8), 26,455 lb (12 000 kg), (Mi-17) 28,660 lb (13 000 kg).

Dimensions: Rotor diam, 69 ft $10\frac{1}{4}$ in (21,29 m); fuselage length (Mi-8), 59 ft $7\frac{3}{8}$ in (18,17 m), (Mi-17) 60 ft $5\frac{3}{8}$ in (18,42 m).

Notes: The Mi-8 (illustrated above) and Mi-17 are fundamentally similar apart from power plant, both providing for a crew of three and 28 passengers in civil versions or 24 passengers on tip-up seats along sidewalls. The first prototype Mi-8 was flown in 1961, series production (Hip-C) commencing in 1963, with more than 10,000 (all versions) since delivered and manufacture continuing (of Mi-17) at a rate of 700 annually. Military versions include the Hip-C and -Mi-17 -H assault transports, the communications Hip-D and -G, and the armed Hip-E and -F.

MIL MI-14PL (HAZE-A)

Country of Origin: USSR.

Type: Amphibious anti-submarine helicopter.

Power Plant: Two 1,900 shp Isotov TV-3 turboshafts.

Performance: (Estimated) Max speed, 143 mph (230 km/h); max cruise, 130 mph (210 km/h); hovering ceiling (in ground effect), 5,250 ft (1 600 m), (out of ground effect), 2,295 ft (700 m); tactical radius, 124 mls (200 km).

Weights: Max take-off, 28,660 lb (13 000 kg).

Dimensions: Rotor diam, 69 ft 10¼ in (21,29 m); fuselage length, 59 ft 7 in (18,15 m).

Notes: The Mi-14PL amphibious anti-submarine warfare helicopter, which serves with shore-based elements of the Soviet Naval Air Force, is a derivative of the Mi-8 (see page 238) with essentially similar power plant and dynamic components to those of the later Mi-17, and much of the structure is common between the two helicopters. New features include the boat-type hull, outriggers which, housing the retractable lateral twin-wheel undercarriage members, incorporate water rudders, a search radar installation beneath the nose and a sonar "bird" beneath the tailboom root. The Haze-B is a version of the Mi-14PL used for the mine countermeasures task. The Mi-14PL possesses a weapons bay for ASW torpedoes, nuclear depth charges and other stores. This amphibious helicopter reportedly entered service in 1975 and about 140 were in Soviet Navy service by the beginning of 1987, other recipients being Bulgaria, Libya, Cuba, Poland and East Germany.

MIL MI-24 (HIND-D)

Country of Origin: USSR.

Type: Assault and anti-armour helicopter.

Power Plant: Two 2,200 shp Isotov TV3-117 turboshafts.

Performance: (Estimated) Max speed, 170–180 mph (273–290 km/h) at 3,280 ft (1 000 m); max cruise, 145 mph (233 km/h); max inclined climb rate, 3,000 ft/min (15,24 m/sec).

Weights: (Estimated) Normal take-off (with four missiles), 22,000 lb (10 000 kg).

Dimensions: (Estimated) Rotor diam, 55 ft 0 in (16,76 m); fuselage length, 55 ft 6 in (16,90 m).

Notes: By comparison with the Hind-A version of the Mi-24 (see 1977 edition), the Hind-D embodies a redesigned forward fuselage and is optimised for the gunship role, having tandem stations for the weapons operator (in nose) and pilot. The Hind-D can accommodate eight fully-equipped troops, has a barbette-mounted four-barrel rotary-type 12,7-mm cannon beneath the nose and can carry up to 2,800 lb (1 275 kg) of ordnance externally, including four AT-2 Swatter IR-homing anti-armour missiles and four pods each with 32 57-mm rockets. It has been exported to Afghanistan, Algeria, Bulgaria, Cuba, Czechoslovakia, East Germany, Hungary, India, Iraq, Libya, Nicaragua, Poland and South Yemen. The Hind-E is similar but has provision for four laser-homing tube-launched Spiral anti-armour missiles. With the nose gun barbette deleted and replaced by a twin-barrel 30-mm cannon mounted on the starboard fuselage side it is known as Hind-F.

MIL MI-26 (HALO)

Country of Origin: USSR.

Type: Military and commercial heavy-lift helicopter.

Power Plant: Two 11,400 shp Lotarev D-136 turboshafts.

Performance: Max speed, 183 mph (295 km/h); normal cruise, 158 mph (255 km/h); hovering ceiling (in ground effect), 14,765 ft (4 500 m), (out of ground effect), 5,905 ft (1 800 m); range (at 109,127 lb/49 500 kg), 310 mls (500 km), (at 123,457 lb/56 000 kg), 497 mls (800 km).

Weights: Empty, 62,169 lb (28 200 kg); normal loaded, 109,227 lb (49 500 kg); max take-off, 123,457 lb (56 000 kg).

Dimensions: Rotor diam, 104 ft 11⅞ in (32,00 m); fuselage length (nose to tail rotor), 110 ft 7¾ in (33,73 m).

Notes: The heaviest and most powerful helicopter ever flown, the Mi-26 first flew as a prototype on 14 December 1977, production of pre-series machines commencing in 1980, and preparations for full-scale production having begun in 1981. Featuring an innovative eight-bladed main rotor and carrying a flight crew of five, the Mi-26 has a max internal payload of 44,090 lb (20 000 kg). The freight hold is larger than that of the fixed-wing Antonov An-12 transport and at least 70 combat-equipped troops or 40 casualty stretchers can be accommodated. Although allegedly developed to a civil requirement, the primary role of the Mi-26 is obviously military and the Soviet Air Force achieved initial operational capability with the series version late 1983. During the course of 1982, the Mi-26 established new international payload-to-height records. Ten Mi-26 helicopters are being supplied to India.

MIL MI-28 (HAVOC)

Country of Origin: USSR.

Type: Tandem two-seat attack helicopter.

Power Plant: Two 2,000–2,500 shp turboshafts (possibly related to the Isotov TV3-117).

Performance: (Estimated) Max speed, 186 mph (300 km/h); tactical radius, 149 mls (240 km).

Weights: No details available for publication.

Dimensions: (Estimated) Rotor diam, 55 ft 9 in (17,00 m); fuselage length (including tail rotor), 57 ft 1 in (17,40 m).

Notes: Development of the Mi-28 (the above illustration of which should be considered as provisional) is believed to have commenced in the early 'eighties, and it is expected to be deployed by attack helicopter regiments during the course of 1987. The Mi-28 has a single large-calibre gun (probably a multi-barrel 23-mm weapon) in an undernose barbette, and pylons beneath each stub wing are expected to carry pods each containing four laser-guided anti-armour missiles, plus tube-launched missiles for air-air or air-ground use at their tips. The Mi-28 is closely comparable in size and performance capability with the AH-64 Apache, and, unlike the Mi-24 (Hind), possesses no transport capability, design emphasis having apparently been placed on agility and survivability. The structure is believed to embody integral armour around the area of the tandem cockpits, and noteworthy features include the pod-mounted engines with upward deflected jet pipes. The Mi-28 is equipped with infra-red suppressors and infra-red decoy dispensers.

PZL SWIDNIK W-3 SOKOL

Country of Origin: Poland.
Type: Multi-purpose and transport helicopter.
Power Plant: Two 870 shp PZL-10W turboshafts.
Performance: (At 13,448 lb/6 100 kg) Max speed, 160 mph (257 km/h); max cruise, 146 mph (235 km/h); econ cruise, 137 mph (220 km/h); max inclined climb, 1,673 ft/min (8,5 m/sec); hovering ceiling (in ground effect), 8,695 ft (2 650 m), (out of ground effect), 6,235 ft (1 900 m); range (no reserves), 444 mls (715 km), (with auxiliary fuel), 761 mls (1 225 km).
Weights: Operational empty, 8,002 lb (3 630 kg); max take-off, 14,000 lb (6 350 kg).
Dimensions: Rotor diam, 51 ft 6 in (15,70 m); fuselage length, 46 ft 3 in (14,10 m).
Notes: The first of five prototypes of the Sokól (Falcon) was flown on 16 November 1979, the development programme being delayed while various design changes were introduced, flight trials being resumed on 6 May 1982. Production of a pre-series of Sokól helicopters was initiated in 1985, with operational testing commencing late 1986, and full-scale production being scheduled to commence during 1987. The Sokól accommodates 12 passengers or, in the aeromedical role, four casualty stretchers and a medical attendant. In the cargo role up to 4,409 lb (2 000 kg) may be carried internally, and both commercial and military versions are proposed. The PZL-10W engines are Polish derivatives of the Soviet Glushenkov TVD-10.

SIKORSKY CH-53E SUPER STALLION

Country of Origin: USA.
Type: Amphibious assault transport helicopter.
Power Plant: Three 4,380 shp General Electric T64-GE-415 turboshafts.
Performance: (At 56,000 lb/25 400 kg) Max speed, 196 mph (315 km/h) at sea level; cruise, 173 mph (278 km/h) at sea level; max inclined climb, 2,750 ft/min (13,97 m/sec); hovering ceiling (in ground effect), 11,550 ft (3 520 m), (out of ground effect), 9,500 ft (2 895 m); range, 1,290 mls (2 075 km).
Weights: Empty, 33,226 lb (15 071 kg); max take-off, 73,500 lb (33 339 kg).
Dimensions: Rotor diam, 79 ft 0 in (24,08 m); fuselage length, 73 ft 5 in (22,38 m).
Notes: The CH-53E is a growth version of the CH-53D Sea Stallion (see 1974 edition) embodying a third engine, an uprated transmission system, a seventh main rotor blade and increased rotor diameter. The first of two prototypes was flown on 1 March 1974, and the first of two pre-production examples followed on 8 December 1975, production of two per month being divided between the US Navy and US Marine Corps at beginning of 1987, against total requirement for 160 through 1992. The CH-53E can accommodate up to 55 troops in a high-density seating arrangement. Fleet deliveries began mid-1981, and the first production example of the MH-53E Sea Dragon (illustrated) mine countermeasures version (35 required by US Navy) was delivered in June 1986.

SIKORSKY S-70C

Country of Origin: USA.

Type: Commercial transport helicopter.

Power Plant: Two 1,625 shp General Electric CT7-2C turboshafts.

Performance: Econ cruise speed, 186 mph (300 km/h); max inclined climb rate, 2,770 ft/min (14,1 m/sec); service ceiling, 17,200 ft (5,240 m); hovering ceiling (in ground effect), 8,700 ft (2 650 m), (out of ground effect), 4,800 ft (1 460 m); range (standard fuel with reserves), 294 mls (473 km) at 155 mph (250 km/h) at 3,000 ft (915 m), (max fuel without reserves), 342 mls (550 km).

Weights: Empty, 10,158 lb (4 607 kg); max take-off, 20,250 lb (9 185 kg).

Dimensions: Rotor diam, 53 ft 8 in (16,36 m); fuselage length, 50 ft 0¾ in (15,26 m).

Notes: The S-70C is a commercial derivative of the H-60 series of military helicopters, and may be configured for a variety of utility missions, such as maritime and environmental survey, mineral exploration and external lift, provision being made for an 8,000-lb (3 629-kg) capacity external cargo hook. Options include a winterisation kit, a cabin-mounted rescue hoist and an aeromedical evacuation kit. The S-70C has a flight deck crew of two and can accommodate 12 passengers in standard cabin configuration or up to 19 passengers in high density layout. Twenty-four were being delivered to China during 1985, and 14 were ordered during 1986 by the Nationalist Chinese Air Force of Taiwan.

SIKORSKY S-70 (UH-60A) BLACK HAWK

Country of Origin: USA.

Type: Tactical transport helicopter.

Power Plant: Two 1,543 shp General Electric T700-GE-700 turboshafts.

Performance: Max speed, 224 mph (360 km/h) at sea level; cruise, 166 mph (267 km/h); vertical climb rate, 450 ft/min (2,28 m/sec); hovering ceiling (in ground effect), 10,000 ft (3 048 m), (out of ground effect), 5,800 ft (1 758 m); endurance, 2·3-3·0 hrs.

Weights: Design gross, 16,500 lb (7 485 kg); max take-off, 22,000 lb (9 979 kg).

Dimensions: Rotor diam, 53 ft 8 in (16,23 m); fuselage length, 50 ft 0¾ in (15,26 m).

Notes: The Black Hawk was winner of the US Army's UTTAS (Utility Tactical Transport Aircraft System) contest. The first of three YUH-60As was flown on 17 October 1974, and a company-funded fourth prototype flew on 23 May 1975. The Black Hawk is primarily a combat assault squad carrier, accommodating 11 fully-equipped troops. Variants include the EH-60A ECM model, deliveries of which commenced late 1985, and the HH-60A Night Hawk rescue helicopter. The USAF is expected to procure 90 HH-60s and 77 EH-60s. The first production deliveries of the UH-60A to the US Army were made in June 1979, with some 800 delivered by beginning of 1987 against requirement for 1,107. The RAAF ordered 14 (against requirement for 48) of the S-70A-9 export Black Hawk during 1986.

SIKORSKY S-70L (SH-60B) SEA HAWK

Country of Origin: USA.
Type: Shipboard multi-role helicopter.
Power Plant: Two 1,690 shp General Electric T700-GE-401 turboshafts.
Performance: (At 20,244 lb/9 183 kg) Max speed, 167 mph (269 km/h) at sea level; max cruising speed, 155 mph (249 km/h) at 5,000 ft (1 525 m); max vertical climb, 1,192 ft/min (6,05 m/sec); time on station (at radius of 57 mls/92 km), 3 hrs 52 min.
Weights: Empty equipped, 13,678 lb (6 204 kg); max take-off, 21,844 lb (9 908 kg).
Dimensions: Rotor diam, 53 ft 8 in (16,36 m); fuselage length, 50 ft 0¾ in (15,26 m).
Notes: Winner of the US Navy's LAMPS (Light Airborne Multi-Purpose System) Mk III helicopter contest, the SH-60B is intended to fulfil both anti-submarine warfare (ASW) and anti-ship surveillance and targeting (ASST) missions, and the first of five prototypes was flown on 12 December 1979, and the last on 14 July 1980. Evolved from the UH-60A (see page 246), the SH-60B is intended to serve aboard DD-963 destroyers, DDG-47 Aegis cruisers and FFG-7 guided-missile frigates as an integral extension of the sensor and weapon system of the launching vessel. The US Navy has a requirement for 204 SH-60Bs, the first of which was delivered in October 1983, and for 175 simplified SH-60Fs without MAD gear. The Australian Navy has ordered 16 Sea Hawks with deliveries commencing September 1987.

SIKORSKY S-76B

Country of Origin: USA.

Type: Commercial transport helicopter.

Power Plant: Two 960 shp Pratt & Whitney (Canada) PT6B-36 turboshafts.

Performance: (Manufacturer's estimates) Max cruise speed, 167 mph (269 km/h); econ cruise, 155 mph (250 km/h); max inclined climb, 1,700 ft/min (8,63 m/sec); service ceiling, 16,000 ft (4 875 m); hovering ceiling (in ground effect), 8,700 ft (2 650 m), (out of ground effect), 5,900 ft (1 800 m); range (max payload), 207 mls (333 km), (max standard fuel), 414 mls (667 km).

Weights: Empty, 6,250 lb (2 835 kg); max take-off, 11,000 lb (4 989 kg).

Dimensions: Rotor diam, 44 ft 0 in (13,41 m); fuselage length, 43 ft 4½ in (13,22 m).

Notes: The S-76B is a derivative of the S-76 Mk II (see 1984 edition) from which it differs primarily in the type of power plant. A prototype of the S-76B was flown for the first time on 22 June 1984, and first customer deliveries were effected the first half of 1985. Offering a 51 per cent increase in useful load under hot and high conditions by comparison with the S-76 Mk II, the S-76B provides accommodation for a flight crew of two and a maximum of 12 passengers. A total of some 300 S-76 helicopters (all versions) had been delivered by the beginning of 1987. Commercial and military (H-76 Eagle) utility versions are available, a multi-role naval version, the H-76N, being under development.

WESTLAND TT30(30-160)

Country of Origin: United Kingdom.
Type: Transport and utility helicopter.
Power Plant: Two 1,150 shp Rolls-Royce Gem 60-3 turbo-shafts.
Performance: (At max take-off weight) Max continuous cruise speed, 138 mph (222 km/h) at sea level; hovering ceiling (in ground effect), 3,800 ft (1 158 m), (out of ground effect), 2,600 ft (792 m); max ferry range, 403 mls (648 km).
Weights: Operational empty, 6,982 lb (3 167 kg); max take-off, 12,800 lb (5 806 kg).
Dimensions: Rotor diam, 43 ft 8 in (13,31 m); fuselage length, 47 ft 0 in (14,33 m).
Notes: The Westland 30, first flown on 10 April 1979, is an enlarged, twin-engined derivative of the Lynx, featuring an entirely new fuselage offering a substantial increase in capacity. With a crew of two, the Westland 30 offers accommodation for 17 passengers in airline comfort standards, an executive transport version accommodating up to 10 passengers. Utilising more than 85 per cent of the proven systems of the Lynx, the Westland 30 is designed for single-pilot IFR operation, the initial -100 version having Gem 41 engines. At the beginning of 1987, a batch of 21 helicopters was being manufactured for delivery to India for use in support of the Bombay High offshore oil field. The -200 version of the TT30 differs essentially in having General Electric CT7-2B engines similar to those of the TT300 which is described on page 250.

WESTLAND TT300

Country of Origin: United Kingdom.
Type: Military tactical transport helicopter.
Power Plant; Two 1,725 shp General Electric CT7-2B turbo-shafts.
Performance: Max speed, 172 mph (278 km/h) at sea level, max continuous cruise, 155 mph (250 km/h); max range, 345 mls (555 km).
Weights: Max take-off, 16,000 lb (7 258 kg).
Dimensions: Rotor diam, 43 ft 8 in (13,31 m); fuselage length, 47 ft 0 in (14,33 m).
Notes: First flown on 5 February 1986, the TT300 is a more powerful military derivative of the Westland 30 with an entirely new dynamics system. It employed a five-bladed main rotor with blades of advanced design and primarily of composite material, and a five-bladed composite tail rotor. Up to 17 fully-equipped troops may be accommodated, 3,000 lb (1 360 kg) of stores, or up to 6,000 lb (2 722 kg) on an external cargo hook. In the casualty evacuation role, five stretcher cases and six seated wounded may be carried. A commercial version is proposed which will carry a full complement of 17 passengers and their baggage at 166 mph (267 km/h) over a distance of 247 mls (398 km), or, with a long-range tank, 13 passengers and their baggage for 414 mls (667 km). The cockpit is compatible with use of night vision goggles, and EFIS is available as an option. Military variants of the basic Gem-engined helicopter (see page 249) are also proposed as the TT30.

WESTLAND SUPER LYNX

Country of Origin: United Kingdom.
Type: Multi-role maritime helicopter.
Power Plant: Two 1,120 shp Rolls-Royce Gem 42 turbo-shafts.
Performance: Max continuous cruise speed, 161 mph (260 km/h) at sea level; normal inclined climb, 1,970 ft/min (10 m/sec); range (anti-surface vessel role with four ASMs and 20 min reserves), 265 mls (426 km), (search and rescue), 391 mls (630 km).
Weights: Max take-off, 11,300 lb (5 126 kg).
Dimensions: Rotor diam, 42 ft 0 in (12,80 m); length (main rotor folded), 45 ft 3 in (13,79 m).
Notes: Under development at the beginning of 1987 with availability from late 1988, the Super Lynx is the latest development of the Lynx family and is intended to fulfil anti-shipping, anti-submarine and search and rescue roles. The principal new features by comparison with earlier naval Lynx helicopters include a MEL Super Searcher 360 deg radar installation, increased fuel capacity and a redesigned tail rotor. Provision is made to carry up to four Sea Skua, AS 12 or AS 15TT air-to-surface missiles or two long-range Penguin missiles, and in the rescue role the cabin can accommodate eight survivors, or, more typically, three stretcher cases and a medical attendant. Radius of action with three crew, a 600-lb (272-kg) capacity hoist and six survivors is 174 mls (280 km). A total of 342 of the earlier Lynx had been ordered by the beginning of 1987.

WESTLAND SEA KING

Country of Origin: United Kingdom (US licence).
Type: Anti-submarine warfare and search-and-rescue helicopter.
Power Plant: Two 1,465 shp Rolls-Royce Gnome H.1400-1T turboshafts.
Performance: Max speed, 143 mph (230 km/h); max continuous cruise at sea level, 131 mph (211 km/h); hovering ceiling (in ground effect), 5,000 ft (1 525 m), (out of ground effect), 3,200 ft (975 m); range (standard fuel), 764 mls (1 230 km), (auxiliary fuel), 937 mls (1 507 km).
Weights: Empty equipped (ASW), 13,672 lb (6 201 kg), (SAR), 12,376 lb (5 613 kg); max take-off, 21,500 lb (9 752 kg).
Dimensions: Rotor diam, 62 ft 0 in (18,90 m); fuselage length, 55 ft 9¾ in (17,01 m).
Notes: The Sea King Mk 2 is an uprated version of the basic ASW and SAR derivative of the licence-built S-61D (see 1982 edition), the first Mk 2 being flown on 30 June 1974, and being one of 10 Sea King Mk 50s ordered by the Australian Navy. Twenty-one to the Royal Navy as HAS Mk 2s, and 19 examples of a SAR version to the RAF as HAR Mk 3s. Current production version is the HAS Mk 5, delivery of 17 to Royal Navy having commenced October 1980, and a further 13 subsequently being ordered. All HAS Mk 2s being brought up to Mk 5 standards and eight Mks 2 and 3 fitted with Thorn-EMI searchwater radar for airborne early warning duty. The HAS Mk 5 is illustrated above.

INDEX OF AIRCRAFT TYPES

254